Bejeweled

Bejeweled

Beautiful Fashion Jewelry to Make and Wear Using Crystals, Beads, and Charms

Claire Aristides

Photography by Sian Irvine

St. Martin's Griffin
New York

www.stmartins.com

Library of Congress Cataloging-in-Publication Data
available upon request

ISBN-13: 978-0-312-37277-4
ISBN-10: 0-312-37277-9

First published in Great Britain by Jacqui Small
an imprint of Aurum Press
7 Greenland Street
London NW1 0ND

Publisher: **Jacqui Small**
Editorial manager: **Kate John**
Designer: **Lucy Gowans**
Photographer: **Sian Irvine**
Props Stylist: **Stella Nicolaisen**
Editor: **Judith Hannam**
Production: **Peter Colley**

First U.S. Edition: November 2007

10 9 8 7 6 5 4 3 2 1

Printed in China

Contents

Introduction

For me fashion jewelry is an art and passion, and I have written this book to share my passion with you. To create your own designer jewelry is not only a lot of fun, but is also very rewarding. A piece of jewelry makes a statement; a splash of jewelry can frequently complete an outfit.

My love of jewelry started at an early age; being the youngest of four daughters, I adored watching my mom and older sisters dressing up. I still enjoy going through my mom's jewelry box today. As a designer, my personal signature is a love of mixing colors to create beautiful combinations. I often design according to the materials, looking to bring out the most from the beads and stones. You, too, will develop your own personal style and find your own inspirations. Jewelry is an expression of our personality, and I hope you will add your own style when making these designs.

I have selected varieties of necklace, bracelet, and earring designs that are timeless classics, sure to see you through many fashion seasons. From the statement sparkly chandelier earrings and classic charm bracelet to the ribbon and chain necklace, these stylish designs will become key staples in your jewelry box.

Each project includes step-by-step instructions and images to guide you, as well as invaluable tips and tricks of the trade based on my years of jewelry making. Whether you are a beginner or an advanced jewelry artist, each project will provide you with new and exciting skills to develop your jewelry-making techniques. Each project in the book also lists any specific tools and equipment you will need.

I hope you enjoy working through this book as much as I have enjoyed putting it together!

Clare

Getting Started

Basic Materials

Jewelry making may seem daunting at first, but I hope this section will provide you with a clear understanding of the types of components involved and how to use them.

There are literally hundreds of varieties of beads in a wide range of materials – metal, glass (of which there is another wide variety), plastic or acrylic, wood, ceramic, crystal, semiprecious or gemstone, and fabric – and this is not an exhaustive list! There is also an endless choice of colors, sizes, and textures of beads.

Each project in the book lists the specific tools and equipment you will need. Most bead stores and craft stores sell a selection of tools and findings for jewelry making. Speciality bead stores in your local area, as well as stores online are also a fantastic source for the essentials: eBay is great for chains, findings, and mixed bead bags; craft stores for buttons, ribbons, tassels, and suede; fabric stores for ribbon, tassels, buttons, and beads. And don't forget to use old beads from discarded jewelry, or vintage beads and jewelry from flea markets and estate sales, which can make stunning pieces. After a little practice you will find your imagination leads you to use anything and everything.

Organizing your beads is essential and helps in the design process as it enables you to group similar beads together. Most craft stores stock a range of containers with compartments. I suggest either clear or opaque boxes so you can see the beads easily. It's also a good idea is to add a label of what's inside to each box for quick reference.

Before you begin, it is always wise to place your stringing materials and beads in front of you, so you can plan how your finished piece will look. A little bit of planning before you begin is important and will save on unnecessary use of pins and wire. Bead boards are handy as they allow you to arrange your beads precisely and to make sure you have enough to make your desired length. Bead mats are also worthwhile as they prevent beads and findings from rolling off the surface of your workbench. You could use a thin hand towel as an alternative.

Crystal

The wonderful choice of color, shape, and size means that crystal beads are particularly cherished by jewelers and hobbyists.

Crystal is a very high-quality glass that can be colored, cut, and faceted for a brilliant finish, though the term crystal can also refer to colorless semiprecious quartz stone or rock crystal. Crystal glass beads have long been an important component in all jewelry designing and beading, and there is an enormous variety of shapes and sizes available, from round multifaceted, bicone, cube, teardrop, to designer-shaped pendants such as stars, hearts, butterflies, and crosses.

Crystal is made by adding lead oxide to glass. It is this lead content that makes the beads sparkle and reflect colors more vibrantly than plain glass. Crystal is heavier than glass, and the higher the lead content, the better quality the crystal.

Crystal beads can be either faceted machine cut or fire polished. Machine-cut crystals are cut and faceted, much like a precious stone, by a special mechanical process. This results in extremely "sharp" edges on each facet, with each facet identical.

The leading producers of faceted glass beads are found in the Czech Republic and Austria. The most famous producer of crystal components is the Swarovski factory in Watten, Austria. Swarovski crystals are renowned for their high quality and brilliance, the result of being made from a minimum of 32 percent lead.

Swarovski has developed a range of stunning signature colors that duplicate actual gemstone colors such as tanzanite, emerald, and ruby. A Swarovski crystal bead can be further transformed with different finishes or coatings on the bead's surface. An "AB" or Aurora Borealis finish is a coating on the bead to make it iridescent. This sheen on the bead has a rainbow effect.

Crystal bead size is measured in millimeters, starting from as small as 3mm to as large as 22mm. Smaller beads, such as 4mm bicones, are popular in jewelry designs as they are perfect accent beads.

Mixing the different shapes of crystal will give your designs more character.

1 38 x 22mm crystal Strass teardrop 8721. Strass components are produced exclusively by Swarovksi; every Strass component over 18mm in size will have a distinctive Strass trademark etched into the crystal

2 8–12mm emerald and blue zircon Swarovski hearts 6202

3 26x16mm emerald Swarovski leaf 6735

4 20mm crystal Swarovski cross 6866

5 A mix of 3–10mm crystal, crystal AB and Swarovksi crystal rounds (5000)

6 20mm crystal Swarovski star 6714

7 24 x 12mm vitrail medium and crystal Swarovski multi-color teardrops 6100

8 8mm Pacific opal and erinite Swarovski faceted spacers 5040

9 8mm aqua and crystal vitrail medium Swarovski margarites 3700

10 9 x 6mm indicolite Swarovski teardrop 5500

11 6mm crystal AB and 8mm crystal Swarovski cubes 5601

12 13 x 6.5mm and 11 x 5.5mm erinite Swarovski briolette 6010

13 12 x 18mm crystal Swarovski elongated bicones 5205

14 & 15 11 x 5.5mm crystal and aqua Swarovski pendant drops 6000

16 16mm crystal Swarovski flat back sew-on buttons 3240

17 6mm and 12mm silver crystal rondels and 6mm crystal sphere with chatons

18 3–12mm crystal, jet blue, black diamond and crystal Swarovski bicones 5301

19 20mm crystal vitrail medium VM fancy stone 4600

Semiprecious Beads & Gemstones

Semiprecious beads (also called gemstones) come from all over the world, including Afghanistan (ruby), Australia (opal, hematite), Brazil (aquamarine, amethyst, tourmaline, citrine), China (jade), India (green moss agate, carnelian, apatite), Iran (turquoise), Sri Lanka (Iolite, tiger eye) and the United States (turquoise). They also come in a variety of shapes, from round, rectangle, and chip to teardrop and briolette, and are available in various depths of color and hue. They are weighed in either carats (C) or grams (g).

Since they are a natural material, there will often be flaws, such as chips or fine cracks in the stone. Don't be deterred by these, as imperfections add to the character of the bead, and guarantee your jewelry will be unique.

Often stones are faceted to enhance the brilliance and color. Many gemstones are also treated by heat, to improve either their color or clarity. The type and extent of this treatment can affect the value of the stone. Some treatments are widely used and accepted in practice because the resulting gem is stable, while others are not accepted, usually because the resulting gem color is unstable and may revert to the original tone.

Semiprecious beads are my favorite to work with, since their exquisite color and brilliance make for extra-special jewelry. You don't need to use many in your designs to create impact, and it's possible to find plenty of well-priced stones on the internet – I have found some stunning semiprecious stones on eBay that were completely unique.

Many people link a semiprecious stone with their birthday month. Others believe the stones have the power to heal; indeed, many people use stones and crystals for both physical and non-physical healing.

Much like crystals, semiprecious beads come in different shapes and sizes. Some of my favorite gems are:

1, 4, 5 & 6 Amethyst stones
2 Tiny rondel garnet stones
3 Round coral beads
7 & 11 Rondel and oval shape polished garnet stones
8 Pink agate rectangular beads
9 Carved black onyx flower shape
10 Clear oval quartz
12 Faceted round garnet bead
13 Large cherry quartz rectangle pendant
14 Teardrop pink quartz
15 Pink quartz teardrop
16 Blue sunstone rectangles and rondels
17 Small garnet leaf beads
18 Large Chinese yellow quartz teardrop
19 Round, teardrop and rectangle carnelian stones
20 Small round garnet rondels
21 Pink quartz teardrops
22 Pink quartz rondels

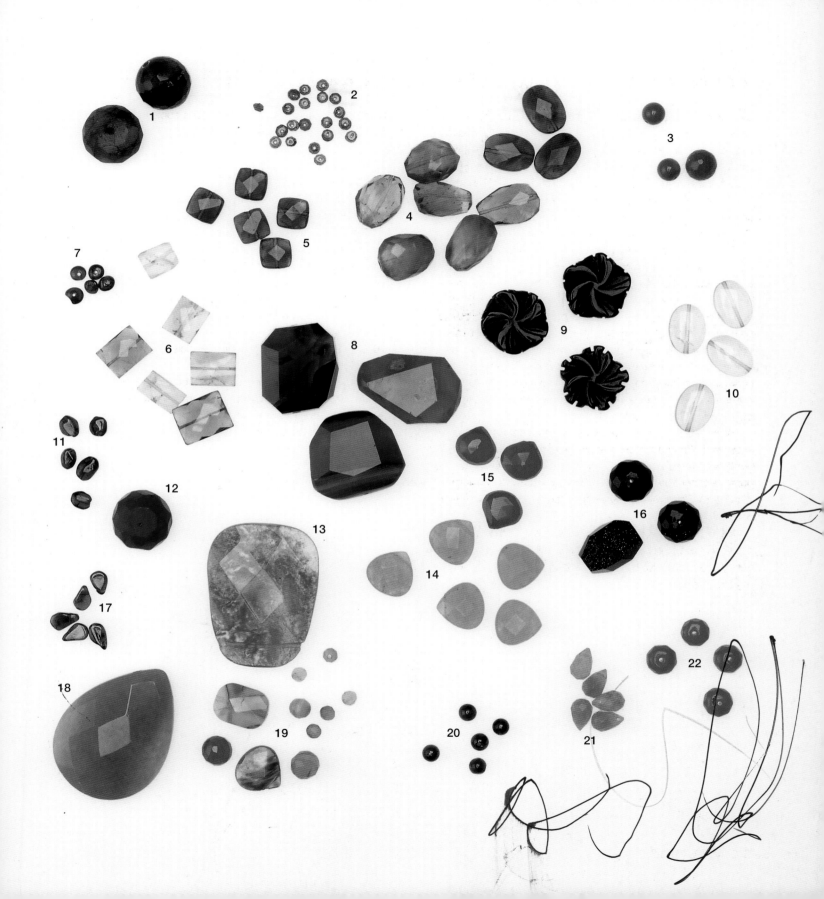

Pearls

Pearls are organic gems formed when a foreign object (i.e., a tiny stone) makes its way into a mollusk's shell, such as that of an oyster.

The most valuable pearls occur naturally and are perfectly symmetrical and large. Natural pearls are produced with no human interference and have a shimmering iridescence. Freshwater pearls originate from mollusks in freshwater lakes and rivers.

Cultured pearls are produced through an artificial process that mimics the organic process of a natural pearl. Often this involves the insertion of a tiny fragment of mother-of-pearl into the mollusk.

There are also baroque pearls (irregularly shaped pearls) and rice pearls (thin ovals), not forgetting seed pearls (tiny pearls), which are wonderful accent beads.

Glass pearl beads are coated with a shimmering finish, that gives a pearllike look and come in standard round bead sizes from 4mm to 12mm. Swarovski has a glass pearl line available in many fashionable colors, including bronze and light green.

Of course, plastic shaped pearls can be a lot of fun, and adding them to your design will help keep down the cost of your piece.

Shell & Abalone

Shells come in a variety of shapes and sizes, including rectangles, ovals, and cubes, as well as large flower designs carved from mother-of-pearl.

Mother-of-pearl is the iridescent coating on the inside of mollusk shells. Most mother-of-pearl has a milky white luster, but it also comes in other colors such as silvery-gray, gray-blue, pink, and salmon.

Paua, which is frequently used for inlay and other decorative purposes, is a member of the abalone family, abalone meaning the "pearly" interior lining of the mollusk of the same name. The paua shell seen on the right is unique to New Zealand and is the most colorful of all the abalone shells, varying in hue from green and pink to purple and blue. Some shells even have a golden or crimson sheen.

Shells and mother-of-pearl are very popular in jewelry design because of their fabulous range of colors and shapes. As they have a summery feel to them, they often feature in designers' summer collections.

Glass

Glass is one of the most frequently used materials for making beads. Glass beads are often categorized by the method used to manipulate the glass.

Probably the earliest beads of true glass were made by what is called the "winding" method. This involves glass being heated to a temperature high enough to make it workable, and then winding it around a steel wire mandrel. The wound bead, while still hot, could be further shaped by manipulating it with graphite, wood, stainless steel, or marble tools and paddles, in a process called "marvering". It could also be pressed into a mold in its molten state. While it is still hot, or after re-heating, the surface of the bead is decorated with fine rods of colored glass, resulting in a type of glass bead called a lampwork bead (one decorated with dots, spirals, and other designs of glass). The bead on the left is a pretty, sterling silver foiled glass, inner flowered lampwork bead.

Modern lampwork beads are now made by using a gas blowtorch to heat a rod of glass and spinning the resulting thread around a metal rod covered in bead release. When the base bead has been formed, other colors of glass can be added to the surface to create many designs. After this initial stage of the beadmaking process, the bead can be further fired in a kiln to make it more durable.

Venetian beads are lampworked from Murano glass. This is a traditional, centuries-old method of making beads from hot glass, and you can still see them being made this way in jewelry workshops on the island of Murano, in Venice, Italy.

The fire-polished process comes from the Czech Republic. It involves the glass bead being pressed in a mold then tumbled in a heated container to polish the facets. This process results in a beautiful, sparkling, slightly rounded, faceted bead that is also scratch-resistant. The edges aren't as "sharp" as those found in machine-cut crystal beads, nor are the facets as evenly sized. If you look very closely, you can tell the difference between a machine-cut and a fire-polished bead, although from a distance it is almost impossible to do so. Not all fire-polished beads are faceted; some, such as bead 6 on the opposite page, are smooth.

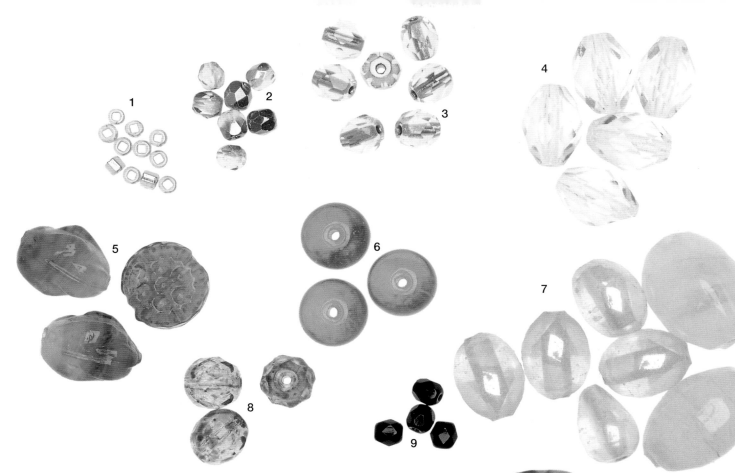

1. Gold-colored seed beads
2. 4mm two-tone fire-polished beads
3. 6mm gold-lined glass round beads
4. 12 x 9mm fire-polished clear oval beads
5. Indian lustered pressed glass brown beads
6. 10mm brown pressed glass round beads
7. 10x7mm lustered glass clear oval beads and 16x12mm Indian glass oval beads
8. 8mm Picasso faceted brown beads (special lustrous finish glass bead)
9. 4mm fire-polished jet beads
10. 15x13mm Venetian-style oval beads
11. Indian lustered pressed glass black beads

Acrylic

Acrylic beads are striking because of their fabulous shapes and sizes, yet they are not expensive. As a result they have been popular in jewelry design for many years. I often use them to add an unusual shape, as they are available in pyramid, cube, round, chandelier and teardrop shapes, as well as a wide selection of colors.

The Acrylic Flower and Ribbon Necklace – a simple knotted bead and knotted ribbon necklace, shown on page 120 – uses acrylic beads in three sizes, and is a fantastic necklace that looks wonderful when worn.

The beautiful necklace to the left is another design that uses acrylic beads – this time teardrop-shaped beads – that have been wire-wrapped around a crystal button to create a flower shape.

Wood

Wooden beads are a lot of fun to work with and are particularly popular for summer collections because of their natural and textured feel. They can be used as subtle accent beads, as in the Glass Charm and Crystal Wrap Bracelet variation (page 50), which uses a number of neutral-color 8mm wooden beads mixed with sparkly glass beads. A carved wooden bead is also used in the Bag Charm project (page 138). Large wooden beads are popular for necklaces, where the effect can be striking.

A particular appeal of wood is the number of unusual shapes available, as shown in the image above. Another attraction is the variety of colors; one of the first projects in the bracelet section is the Wooden Stretch Bracelet (page 44), which is a striking hot pink color.

Fabric

Fabric beads are also great fun, as the variety of texture and color is enormous. Many jewelry designers' summer ranges feature fabulous crocheted beaded necklaces, which are rich in color and patterns. I have used several fabric beads on the Chunky Charm Bracelet variation (page 54), which add a new dimension to this metal and precious gem bracelet.

People are often reluctant to work with fabric beads because they worry about their durability. Like all fabric, it is best to spray with a fabric protector to help extend the life of your design.

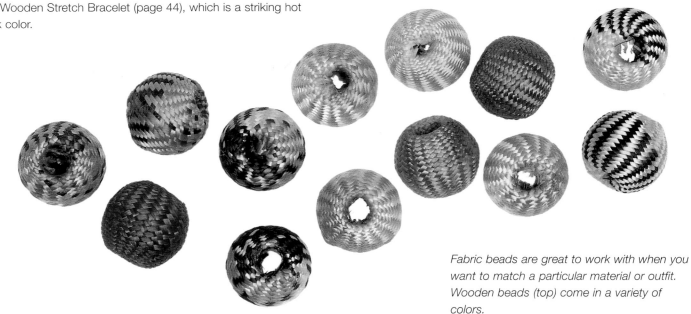

Fabric beads are great to work with when you want to match a particular material or outfit. Wooden beads (top) come in a variety of colors.

Metal

The variety of metal beads and charms is truly astonishing – the selection of gold and silver charms shown here is only a handful of the thousands of metal beads available. It's possible to find everything from butterflies, sailboats, and shell shapes to zodiac charms; in fact, you will be spoiled for choice.

Adding metal beads and charms to bracelets is a popular and effective design touch, and like many designers, I love to work with them. Metal beads also add density, since, in addition to looking fantastic, they add a lovely jingling sound and movement. The Chunky Charm sterling silver bracelet (page 52) is dripping in unusual metal beads that give the bracelet a life of its own.

A long pendant necklace with a mix of metal charms is a staple part of my jewelry box. I try to hunt down unusual metal beads for my designs, taking charms from discarded, pre-loved jewelry or from markets, as they make a piece truly unique. Like all the metal in jewelry making, beads and charms are available in base metal, sterling silver, and gold vermeil, and the price varies accordingly.

Use large metal beads, such as the flower-shaped metal bead shown right, as feature beads.

Tools

There are three key tools that are essential to get you started: chain- (or needle-) nose pliers, side cutters, and round-nose pliers. As you progress and become more experienced, you will want to add crimpers and mandrels to your toolbox. Always buy the best tools you can afford, as good quality ones will last longer and help you make better quality jewelry.

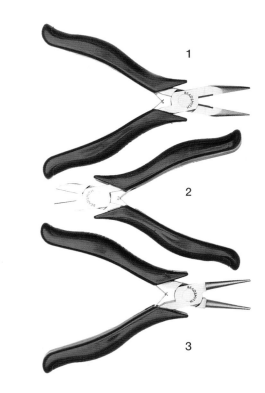

1 Chain-nose/Needle-nose pliers

This tool, which has a smooth, tapered flat nose, is used for straightening and bending wire, as well as for crimping and closing loops. It is used regularly when making jewelry with wire. Avoid using pliers with ridges, which can leave unwanted imprints on your metal.

2 Wire cutters/Side cutters

A good pair of cutters is also very important, as they are used to take apart jewelry and to cut chain, wire, and headpins. The thickness of the wire or chain you are cutting will determine whether you use soft wire cutters or hard wire cutters. When cutting memory wire, use memory wire shears.

3 Round-nose pliers

These are used for making wire loops, so are often used when making earrings. If you look down the barrel of this tool, you will see that it has two graduated cones used for making various sized loops. Where you place your wire on the barrel will determine the size of the loop.

Crimper

A fourth tool you might like to have as you advance is a crimper, which is used to squeeze crimp beads flat. Although chain-nose pliers will suffice when you are starting, a crimper tool will give your crimp beads a neater finish.

Mandrels

Similar to round-nose pliers, but on a larger scale, mandrels are a barrellike graduating cone. They are available in different sizes. By using a mandrel to wrap your wire around, you will be able to create perfectly shaped loops, giving your designs a consistent look. To check sizing you may also like to use a ring sizer.

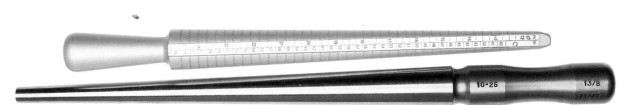

Findings

Findings are the core parts used to make jewelry and include head pins, clasps, jump rings, and crimps. Listed below are some of the most common findings you will use.

1 Jump rings

Circular metal rings of varying size, thickness (gauge), and type of metal that can be used in a variety of ways. An open jump ring is one that can be pulled apart and used to attach two other rings or link chain together. A closed jump ring is a soldered round ring without an opening that is often used for bracelet ends or to hang charms on a pendant. A spilt ring is a tightly coiled ring, like a miniature version of a key ring.

2 Crimps

Small hollow metal beads through which stringing material is threaded; they are then squeezed shut with a crimping tool or chain-nose pliers. Crimps are an important finding to attach stringing materials to a clasp and ring.

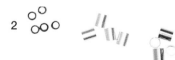

3 Bail

A bail is a component that connects a pendant to a necklace. You can create your own bails using wire.

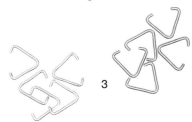

4 Bead tips

Also called callotes, bead tips are used to finish necklaces strung with thread or cord. To use them, bring your thread through the hole, into the clamshell part of the bead tip. Tie a knot to keep the bead tip tight against your last bead. Add a small drop of glue and close the clamshell with pliers. Add your clasp to the bead tip, using an open jump ring, then close it with pliers.

Head pins

Headpins are the basis of wire jewelry making, and are used to create connections and join beaded parts together. They vary in length and width, and are made in all types of metal. The Charm Bracelet (page 52) is a great example of how to work with them and the impact they can have on your designs.

A standard head pin (**5**) is a small thin pin, similar to a normal sewing pin at the end. A ball pin (**2** and **4**) has a small ball at the end and is thus more decorative than a standard head pin.

Using decorative head pins, such as Bali sterling silver (**3**) and vermeil pins will add an ornamental finish to your designs. Eye pins (**1**) have a loop at the end and can be used to make connections to a clasp, chain, or another eye pin.

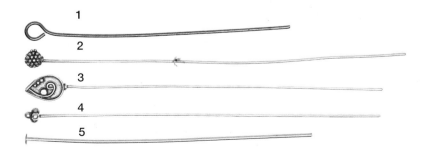

Components

There is a wide variety of components or findings you can use when creating earrings. Depending on the occasion or your particular fancy, you can make everything from large, dangly statement earrings to discreet, delicate studs.

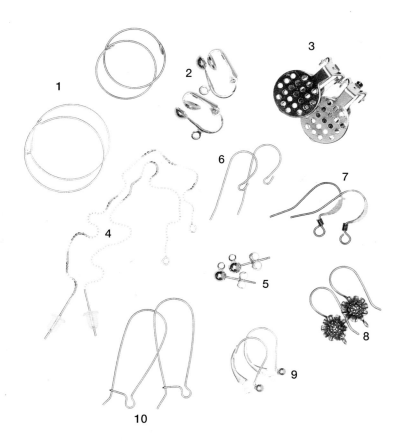

Earrings

Hoop earrings (**1**) are made of hollow wire (also called chenier), which has a fine wire end that is inserted through the ear lobe and then into the hollow part of the wire to forma complete circle. In the earring section, there are two fantastic projects (pages 78 and 94) that show you how to decorate hoops with faceted stones and crystals.

Clip-on earrings (**2** and **3**) are very popular when creating vintage-style earrings. I have used the former for the project on page 82. This style has a small loop for wire-wrapping crystals and beads and is perfect for converting pierced styles to clip-ons. The small holes in the latter allow you to attach crystals and beads to the pad of the earring.

Box chain earrings (**4**) became popular in the 1970s. They come in d i fferent lengths and allow you to add a cluster to the bottom loop.

Ball and pin earrings (**5**) have a straight post at the back that goes through the earlobe and is held on with a butterfly end. Again, you can add chain and beaded segments to the main ring to embellish this component.

French earwire earrings (**6**, **7** and **8**), also known as fish-hook earrings, are available in many varieties, but are mainly constructed from an S-shape of wire. Kidney-shaped hooks (**9** and **10**) are similar, with earring **10** being an oversized variation.

Chandelier components

These beautiful components (see above right) are frequently used with earring findings to create stunning, statement earrings, such as the Filigree Chandilier Earrings on page 96. In fact, there are so many fantastic chandelier parts available now that you will be spoiled for choice. They come with a varying number of holes, and in a variety of shapes, metal colors, and sizes. In addition to being used to make elaborate earrings and necklace pendants, they can also be used when joining beaded segments together to create unusual connecting parts.

Brooches & Rings

Brooch and ring components come with a varying number of rings, from 3-hole to 7-hole. They are also available in a variety of metals. See the various ring and brooch projects for more styles and ideas.

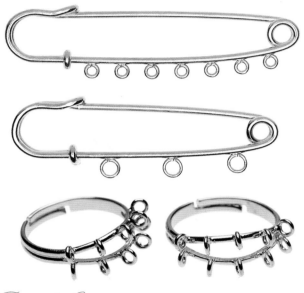

Bead Caps

Decorative cup-shaped components used either side of a bead to add a decorative finish, making your design more complete.

Clasps

Clasps are used to attach two ends of a necklace or bracelet. They come in a variety of shapes, sizes, and mechanics. Some of the more popular include:

Lobster claw

As its name suggests, these clasps (**20**, **21**, and **25**) resemble the claw of a lobster. A small spring keeps the arm closed. Image **26** is a large lobster clasp that you would use for a key ring or bag charm. They are also sometimes referred to as trigger clasps. They come in various sizes and shapes, such as an oval or heart.

Spring ring/Bolt ring

A spring ring, also called a bolt ring (**24**), is a hollow circular metal fastening ring with a spring opening that keeps the arm of the clasp closed.

Toggle clasp

Also referred to as a bar and ring clasp, a toggle clasp (**10**, **15**, **16**, and **17**) works by having a bar (a T-shape) that loops into a ring (an O-shape) to fasten the two ends of jewelry together. They are available in a variety of designs, including heart and flower shapes.

Box clasp

Box clasps (**2**, **3**, **6**, **9**, **14**, and **18**) have a springy tension that holds and aligns the two parts of the box together. One side of the box fits into the other. This type of mechanism is available in round shape and multistrand box clasps, and they often come in a filigree design or with pearls and crystals. Image 13 is an example of an oval-shaped filigree clasp.

Multistrand clasp

Multistrand clasps allow you to add multiple rows to your design. Illustrated here are a sterling silver 3-row, 2-part clasp (**22**) and a vintage-style fan, 3-row clasp (**4**).

Barrel clasp

The two pieces of this clasp screw together to resemble a barrel (**24**). There is a wonderful variety of barrel clasps available, some of which are decorated with crystals or sparkly rhinestones (**11**).

Hook and eye clasp

A straightforward clasp that, at its most simple, consists of a hook and a circular piece that the hook latches onto to secure. There is also a wide range of very pretty and decorative hook and eye clasps available (**1**), including some with filigree detail in vermeil and sterling silver (**23** and **27**) as well as small extender chains, to the end of which you could wire wrap a bead.

S-clasp

A simple version of a hook and eye clasp, S-clasps (**12** and **19**) work by hooking each end of the clasp onto an open ring.

Magnetic clasp

Magnetic clasps (**8**) are popular because they are very easy to use. A small magnetic mechanism exists within the clasp to keep it closed.

Padlock clasp

Padlock clasps work by the arm of the clasp locking into a secure latch on the body of the clasp. Shown here is a sterling silver heart padlock clasp (**5**).

Stringing Components

Wire

Wire is used to join beads to chain, earring findings, clasps, and much more. It comes in a variety of different gauges (thicknesses) – the lower the gauge, the thicker the wire. At first, wire work can be very difficult, but practice will make perfect, and soon you will find yourself wanting to wire-work everything!

It's possible to get copper, brass, or colored wire, as well as plated wire, sterling silver and gold-filled wire. The gauge you use will vary according to the size of your bead and what you are creating. Use the following as a guide:

Gauge guide

14–16 gauge: 1.5–1.2mm/very thick wire
Used for larger holed beads; you will need heavy-duty tools.

18 gauge: 1.0mm/medium thick wire
Used when making your own components. It is perfect for wire-wrapping beads with large holes.

20–22 gauge: 0.8–0.7mm/medium wire
Ideal for wire work with crystals and medium-sized beads. Most base metal head pins and earring posts are made with this wire.

24–26 gauge: 0.6–0.5mm/thin wire
Perfect for wiring delicate semiprecious beads and small pearls to fine chain or chandelier components.

28–30 gauge: 0.4mm/delicate, fine wire
Used for fine wire-wrapping projects. If you work with it regularly, you may find you need wire straightening pliers, which will smooth out any kinks in the wire.

Memory wire

Sturdy, stainless steel wire that never loses its round shape, hence the name memory wire. Available in ring, bracelet, and necklace sizes. Designers often cut the coils of memory wire into individual pieces to be strung with beads and finished with end caps.

Stretch magic elastic

A fantastic material for creating versatile stretch bracelets to fit all size wrists. It is available in a range of colors, although clear elastic is used most often. It also comes in different thickness, so be sure to match the size of bead hole to the thickness of elastic.

Tigertail/Nylon-coated wire

Tigertail is a strong jewelry wire made of multiple strands of steel that are wound together and then coated with nylon, which is often colored. Tigertail can be quite stiff and has a tendency to kink. Alternatively, use soft-flex wire, which is more flexible and less prone to kinking.

Translucent monofilament cord

Essentially fishing nylon, this clear cord is a popular choice when making necklaces and bracelets, as it is very strong and extremely durable.

Chain

Chain is an important component when creating jewelry, though it's not always necessary to use a large amount – using small segments of gold or silver chain to connect sections of beads together and mixing different types of chain together can be very effective.

The range of chain available is tremendous, and it comes in a wide choice of different designs, including traditional cables, as well as a variety of thicknesses.

Chain is traditionally measured in millimeters, though many suppliers will also sell it by the foot. It is available in the following metals:

Gunmetal – chain that has been oxidized by adding a patina/colorant solution to the base metal to turn it a dark black color.

Silver-plated – electroplated base metal covered with between 0.15–0.25 mm of sterling silver.

Sterling silver – this is defined as 92.5 percent pure silver and 7.5 percent copper or other alloys.

Gold-plated – electroplate base metal covered with between 0.15–0.25 mm of gold.

Gold-filled – made by applying multiple layers of carat gold over a base metal chain.

Vermeil – differs from gold-filled in that a heavy electroplating of gold is applied over sterling silver, not a base metal.

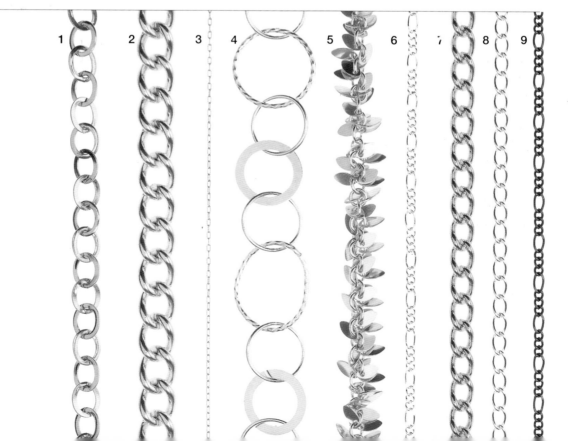

Chains

1 Gold-filled link chain
2 Silver-plated large link chain
3 Gold-filled 1.4mm cable chain
4 Sterling silver hammered decorative chain
5 Sterling silver fancy leaf chain
6 Silver-plated figaro chain
7 Gold-plated large link chain
8 Silver-plated medium link chain
9 Gunmetal figaro chain

1   2   3   4   5   6   7   8   9

Thread

There's no end to what can be used to string beads – thread, nylon, wire, monofilament, ribbon, suede, leather, silk, and cotton to name just a few. I have used many of these in the projects included in this book, so you will get a good understanding of how to work with them. Whatever material you use, however, one of the most important considerations is to make sure it will fit through the bead's hole!

Thread is a very popular choice for stringing pearls and beads. Silk is best for pearls and delicate semiprecious stones, as it will insure your finished necklace drapes more gracefully. Nylon thread is more suited to glass beaded necklaces; it is not as expensive and tends to be more resilient.

Your local craft store should stock both silk and nylon thread in a variety of colors so you can match the thread to your beads or, alternatively, use a contrasting color for a striking effect.

When choosing thread, you need a weight that is thin enough to allow you to thread through the beads, but also heavy enough to form a knot so that the bead is secure. If your thread is too thin, double it or create double knots, so the knot is large enough. You can use this same technique with ribbon and very large-holed beads. Again, check your ribbon will fit through the bead hole.

A beading needle is a flexible twist of fine stainless steel wire that can be threaded in the same way as a sewing needle. It allows you to string very small beads or beads with small holes on your thread more easily.

Ribbons can add a fabulous decorative touch to your designs. One idea is to weave it through the links of chain. Satin ribbon is a particularly good choice for this since it has a long-lasting sheen. Ribbons are perfect, too, for adding bows. I have used satin ribbon to create the decorative bow on the lovely Pearl Stretch Bracelet. In addition, it can be used to attach tassels and buttons to add a unique and decorative finish to your jewelry.

Suede is a fabulous alternative for looping through chain, and leather for knotting through, or creating knots, between beads.

Left: The faux leather flower brooch looks wonderful wire-wrapped to the necklace on page 110. Right: A selection of threads.

Key Techniques

This section explains the key techniques needed when making jewelry. You should refer back to this section whenever you require further detail, or explanation, on a key technique listed in a project.

Attaching clasps to chain with jump rings

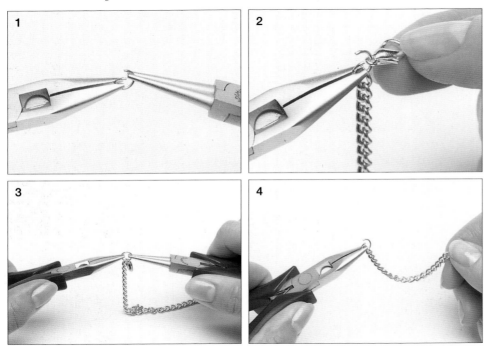

1 & 2 Using pliers, pull apart an open jump ring, then loop it through the last link of the chain and the ring of the clasp.
3 Firmly close the ring so that the clasp and chain are now connected.
4 If using a two-part clasp, pull apart another open jump ring using pliers and loop it through the other end of the chain. Join this jump ring to the matching part of the clasp. If using a lobster clasp, add a closed jump ring.

Cutting chain & standard lengths

Bracelets are usually 7 to 8 inches in length, including the clasp, and necklaces 16 to 24 inches. Before you begin cutting, measure the length of chain you require. If necessary, you can defer cutting it until the very last step as a precaution; just make sure you add some kind of marker to the link of chain where you later want to cut. Keep any small strips of chain for making chain tassels or for connecting parts together.

Creating rosary loops

Loops are the foundation of all wire work, and to create jewelry using wire you must learn how to make them. The easiest to begin with are rosary loops.

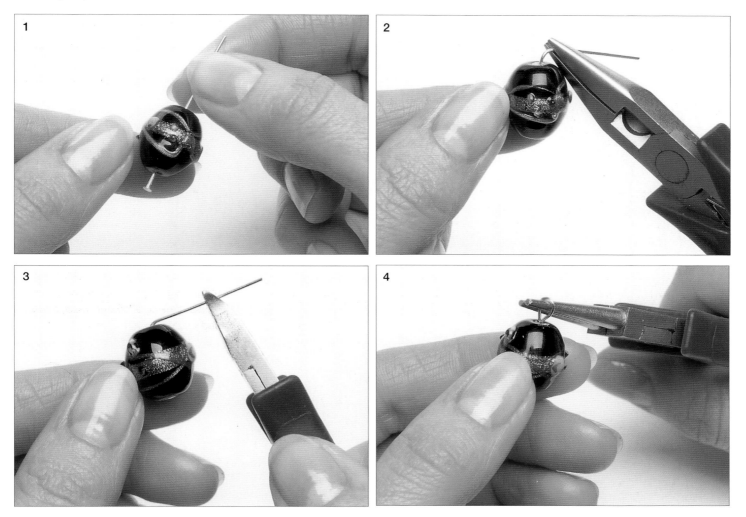

You will need

Head pins or jewelry wire (refer to the wire gauge guide on page 30 to select the correct thickness of wire for your beads)
Chain-nose pliers
Wire cutters
Round-nose pliers

1 Place your bead onto a head pin.
2 Take the chain-nose pliers and bend the head pin at a 90-degree angle.
3 Using cutters, cut the head pin approximately 1 inch along from the bend.
4 Take the round-nose pliers and bend the head pin back on itself to make a loop.

Creating wire-wrapped loops

Wrapped loops are used when wiring beads together, joining segments of beaded parts or dangling a pendant from a necklace, so it is a very useful technique to learn. Wrapping wire is more difficult and takes longer to master than rosary loops, but it is well worth the effort as it prevents loops opening up, which can sometimes happen when you rosary loop wire. It is best to practice first with copper or plated wire, rather than sterling silver or gold-filled wire, which is much more expensive.

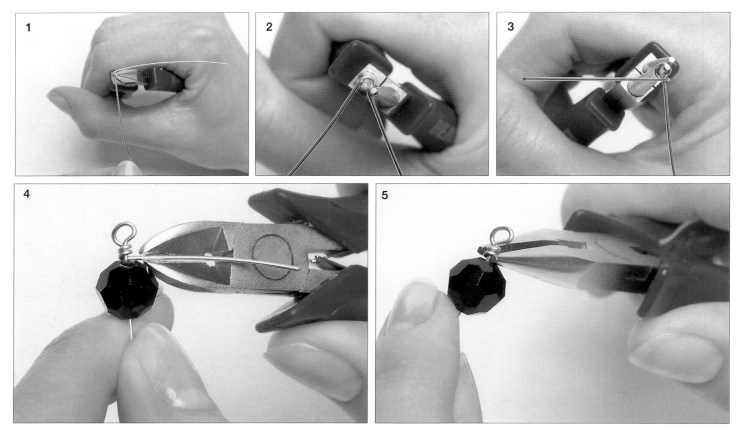

1 Using cutters, cut about 12 inches of wire. About 3 inches from one end, bend it, using chain-nose pliers, to create a 90-degree angle.
2 Place the round-nose pliers at the point of the bend, and then bend the wire away

from yourself to create a loop.
3 Loop the shorter length of wire around the base of the loop.
4 Add the bead to the wire, and hold it in place with your fingers as you wrap the wire. Wrap until there is no wire left. Using

the wire cutters, clip off any excess wire.
5 Using the chain-nose pliers, gently press the loop so it is neat and there are no gaps in the wire.

You will need

Wire cutters

Chain-nose pliers

Round-nose pliers

Head pins or jewelry wire (refer to the wire gauge guide on page 30 to select the correct thickness of wire for your beads)

6

6 If you want to make linked jewelry, you will need to connect the wrapped loops before you close them. To do this, loop the chain or a beaded segement onto the wire before you finish the loop.

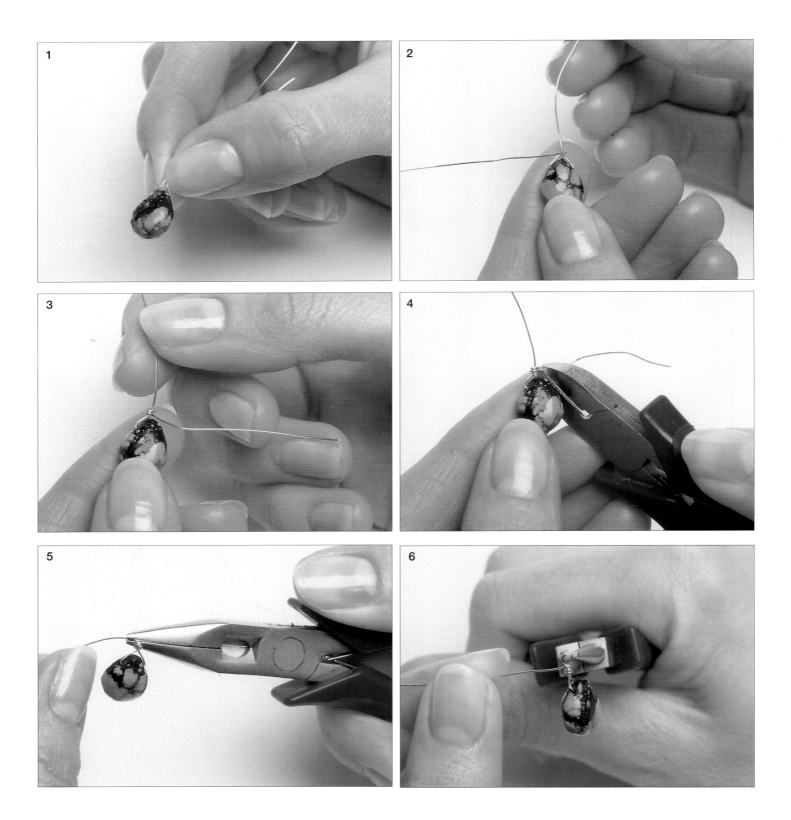

Wire-wrapping top-drilled beads such as teardrops and briolettes

1 Cut approximately 4¹/₂ inches of wire. Place the teardrop through the wire, leaving 1¹/₄ to 1¹/₂ inches of wire at the end. Pinch the two ends of wire together at the top of the teardrop to form a triangle shape, ensuring the teardrop is centered.

2 & 3 Wrap the shorter end of wire around the larger end twice.

4 Snip off the excess shorter wire.

5 Place the chain-nose pliers at the top of the triangle. Bend the long wire at a 90-degree angle.

6 Switch to the round-nose pliers. Bring the end of the wire up and over the pliers to create a loop centered above the teardrop. Twist the wire around the bottom of the loop. Wrap the remaining wire around the space between the loop and the top of the wire triangle. Snip off excess wire and use the chain-nose pliers to tuck the end of the wire under the wrapped cone for a neat finish.

Bead Holes

Beads come in all shapes and sizes and it is important to learn how to work with different types. Bead size is measured in millimeters and they start from as small as 3mm and go up to as large as 30mm. Typically, you will use beads between 4mm and 16mm in size.

Generally, beads are either top-drilled or side-drilled. Briolette and teardrop-shaped beads are usually top-drilled, whereas pearls and glass beads are side-drilled, with the hole in the middle.

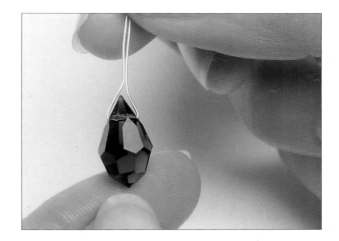

Top-drilled

Side-drilled

Bracelets

Bracelets

Bracelets are one of the most important pieces of jewelry; easily worn both day and night, they make a stylish statement. They are one of my favorite pieces to create, and there is an endless choice of designs.

The ten bracelet projects here are all equally stunning. They cover a wide range of techniques and use a number of different stringing materials and beads. We begin with some starter projects: the Wooden Stretch Bracelet, Heart Bangle, and Glass Charm and Crystal Wrap Bracelet. These provide a great taster of what making jewelry is all about and will allow you to grasp the basics.

We then progress to more difficult designs, with two different styles of charm bracelet. Charm bracelets are often thought of as the ultimate accessory in terms of originality and personality. They date back to the ancient Egyptians, who adorned their bracelets with charms they believed to have supernatural powers. Today charm bracelets have come of age and the term is used loosely to refer to a chain bracelet with an assortment of beads and charms. Take inspiration from our sterling silver Chunky Charm Bracelet (page 52), or you might prefer the more glamorous, semiprecious rondel design.

Finally, we go on to work with different ribbons, threads, and suedes to create the Knotted Chain and Crystal Bracelet (page 62) and the Antique Pearl Bracelet (page 70).

Variations
This a stunning sterling silver semiprecious variation of the bracelet on page 58. The perfectly round circle chain is complemented by large rondel-shaped lapis stones, as well as large Swarovski rhinestone balls (also called Swarovski fireballs or crystal spheres with chatons) and silver metal charms.

Wooden Stretch Bracelet

Much of the fun of making jewelry lies in choosing what components to use and working with different types of beads. In this project it is the rich color of the pink wooden beads that make this such a lovely bracelet.

Materials
Approx. 12 inches stretch elastic
A Glass flower and leaf charms
B Fine plated gold (or silver) chain, approx. 12 inches
C Head pin
D Pink Venetian glass bead
E Small pink wooden beads x 7
F Large pink wooden beads x 6

Tools required
Cutters
Round-nose pliers
Chain-nose pliers
Crimp tool
Superglue

Techniques
Working with elastic; creating tassels.

Tips
If you have cut your elastic already, add a knot to one end to prevent the beads from falling off. Also, there are different sizes of stretch elastic, so be sure to check the elastic will fit through your beads.

1& 2 Add a small wooden bead, then a large one, followed by another small bead, and so on.

3 Add the flower and leaf charms.

4 Using a head pin, create a rosary loop, then add the Venetian bead and the strips of fine chain.

5 Create a loop at the other end of the head pin, making sure the strips of chain are positioned within the loop. This creates the tassel of chain.

6 Double knot the two ends of elastic.

7 Add a drop of superglue to the knot. Once dry, snip the excess elastic with small scissors or cutters.

Another way of finishing your stretch bracelet is to pull both strands of elastic through a crimp bead and then to press the crimp bead with pliers.

Heart Bangle

This project shows you how to embellish a bangle. Bangles are ageless, often simple and classic. I picked up this sterling silver bangle many years ago from a market, originally one of a cluster of six. I've embellished it with a mix of stones and charms. The rose quartz heart is the feature bead and is accompanied by a complementing mix of pearl and charms. The sterling silver flower charm is also delightful, as is the AB crystal through the metal charm, which gives the design some movement. I am a big fan of AB crystals because of their reflective sparkle. I have used the Bali silver pins to tie in with the old darker metal of the bangle. This is a great example of updating old jewelry.

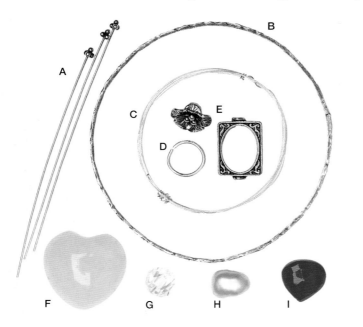

1 Place one of the decorative head pins through the rose-quartz heart pendant and wire-wrap at the top of the pin. See Key Techniques, page 36.
2 Wire-wrap the pink quartz teardrop.
3 Place your head pin through the metal bead, then the crystal to create a charm.
4 Add the remaining beads (pearl and flower charm) to the large jump ring.
5 Loop the open jump ring around the bangle. Close the jump ring firmly to secure the charms to the bangle.

Tips
Refer back to the Key Techniques section before you start, and practice creating a loop on base metal head pins before you use sterling silver pins.

Materials
A Decorative Bali-style sterling silver ball pins
B Sterling silver bangle
C 28 gauge /0.4mm silver wire for wire-wrapping the teardrop pink quartz
D Large silver open jump ring
E Sterling silver metal beads, flower charm (with jump ring attached already), and rectangular metal bead
F Semiprecious heart-shaped rose quartz
G 8mm AB round Swarovski crystal

H Baroque pearl
I Pink quartz teardrop

Tools required
Cutters
Round-nose pliers; chain-nose pliers

Techniques
Create your own charms using head pins.
Attaching an open jump ring to a bangle.

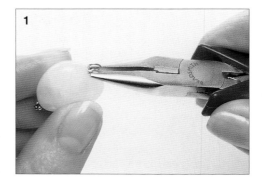

1

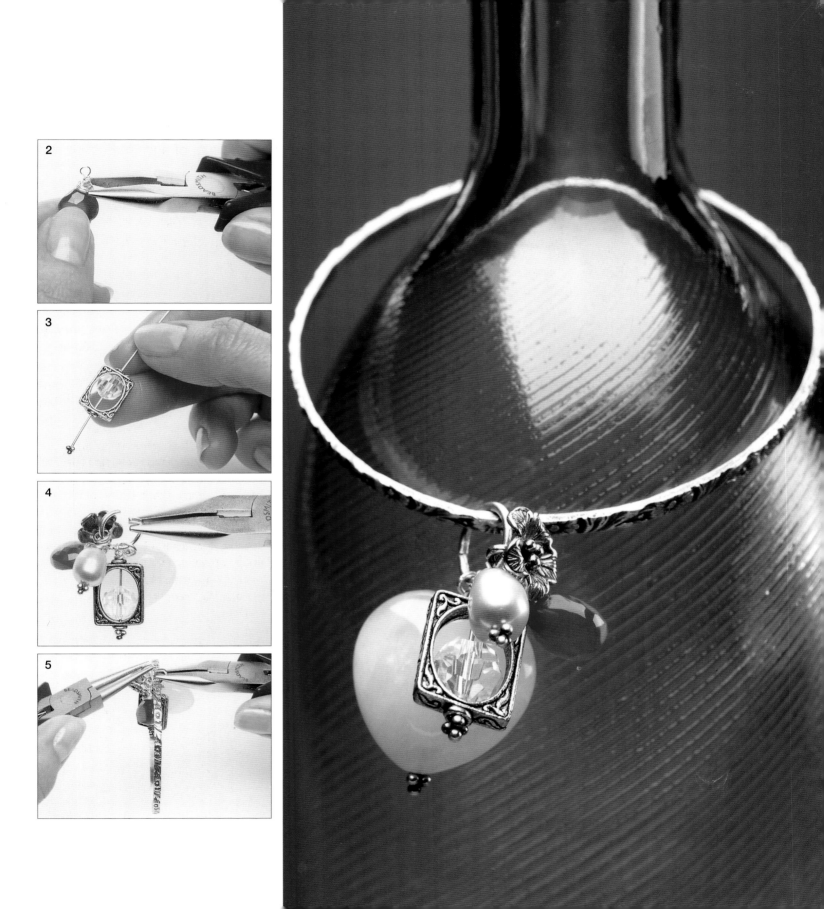

Glass Charm and Crystal Wrap Bracelet

This is an easy project to make, and the finished product looks stunning, demonstrating that it isn't necessary to spend a lot of money to make beautiful jewelry. The bracelet works wonderfully with a random medley of colorful beads. I've selected a mixed bag of purple beads from my local bead store, and added some lovely Swarovski crystals for extra sparkle. The lampwork beads are also particularly beautiful and give the bracelet even more character. Memory wire is a sturdy wire that keeps its shape and looks fantastic with beautiful beads in multiple coils. Memory-wire wrap bracelets are also a lot of fun to wear, as they jiggle around on your wrist.

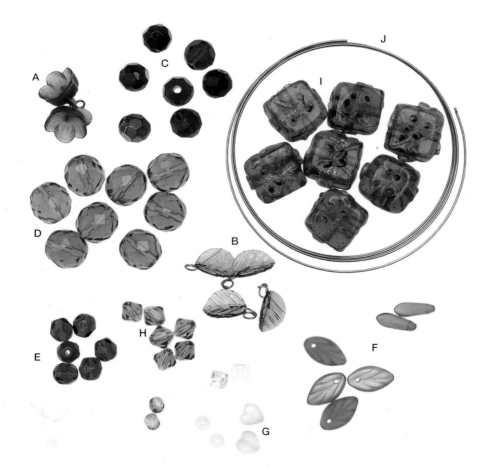

Materials
A & B Flower and leaf charms, approx 10, already on a curled headpin
C, D, E, F, & G Purple glass bead mix, at least 100 beads, including seed beads and a mix of different shapes and sizes of fire-polished glass beads
H Purple 6mm bicone Swarovski crystals, approx. 10
I Purple lampwork beads, approx. 10
J Bracelet size memory wire, at least 6 coils

Tools required
Memory wire cutters
Round-nose pliers

Techniques
Working with memory wire – both cutting and curling the end of it.

How to make the glass charm and crystal wrap bracelet

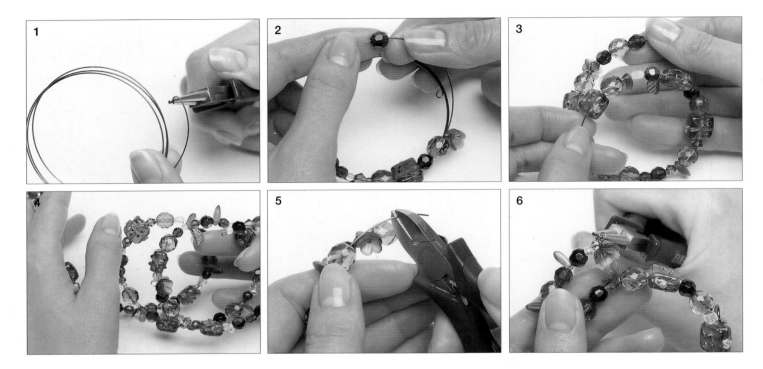

1 If your memory wire is already cut, use round-nose pliers to curl one end of the wire to form a closed loop.

2 Add your beads to the memory wire. Wrap bracelets often work best with no particular pattern to adding your beads.

3 & 4 Continue adding beads until you have at least 5 coils of wire.

5 Once you have your desired number of coils, cut the wire, at least 1 inch from the last bead.

6 Curl the wire with round-nose pliers to create a closed loop.

Tips

Try to leave some slack in the memory wire bracelet, otherwise, it will be too stiff.

You can make as many coils to this bracelet as you like, but bear in mind that too many coils and too many beads will make the bracelet very heavy. Cut the memory wire to your desired number of coils; some craft stores sell memory wire ready cut into coils.

Be sure to use heavy-duty tools when cutting memory wire. I suggest memory wire cutters, which are very sturdy and are designed for cutting this thicker wire.

Variations

You don't need to make this wrap bracelet with as many coils – try two or three coils instead. Or use different beads, such as those used in the wooden wrap bracelet opposite. This bracelet has a wonderful mix of gold metal beads, fire-polished glass beads, wooden beads, gold lampwork heart-shaped charms, plus carved-flower gold dust semiprecious stones. This is an unusual stone with speckles through it.

Chunky Charm Bracelet

One of my favorite bracelets to make is a charm bracelet. What is wonderful about designing a charm bracelet is that you can add any number of different beads and charms to create a unique bracelet full of personality. Often the more mismatched the design, the better the effect.

The feature bead on this bracelet, a kiwi jasper carved into a butterfly shape, makes this a striking design. The other charms on this decorative diamond and circle sterling silver chain, which include Bali-style balls and lantern charms, complement it well. I have also added a gunmetal chain tassel to match the Bali-style silver components.

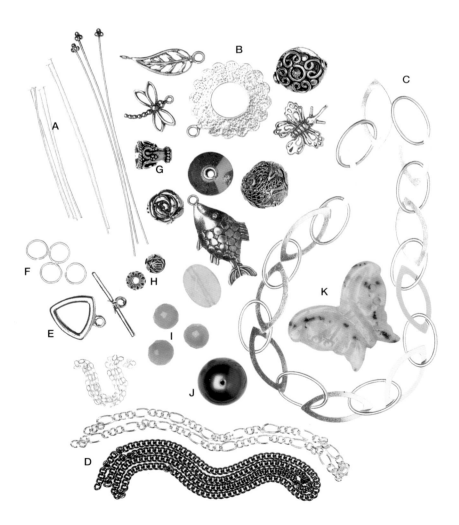

Materials

A A mix of decorative Bali-style sterling head pins, approx. 20
B A mix of Bali-style chunky silver charms: flower, butterfly, round, lantern, oval, leaf
C Diamond and circle shape sterling silver chain, or any large link chain, approx. 12 inches
D A mix of fine silver and gunmetal chains, approx. 8 inches each
E Decorative toggle clasp x 1
F Open jump rings, approx. 10
G Bead cone x 1
H A mix of silver decorative beadcaps and balls, approx. 10
I Amazonite round and oval shapes x 3
J Large pearl, 14mm
K Carved butterfly in kiwi jasper x 1
28 gauge/0.4mm silver wire (optional)

Tools required

Wire cutters
Chain-nose pliers; round-nose pliers

Techniques

Creating chain tassels.
Attaching bead cones to chain.
Attaching charms to chain with open jump rings.

How to make the chunky charm bracelet

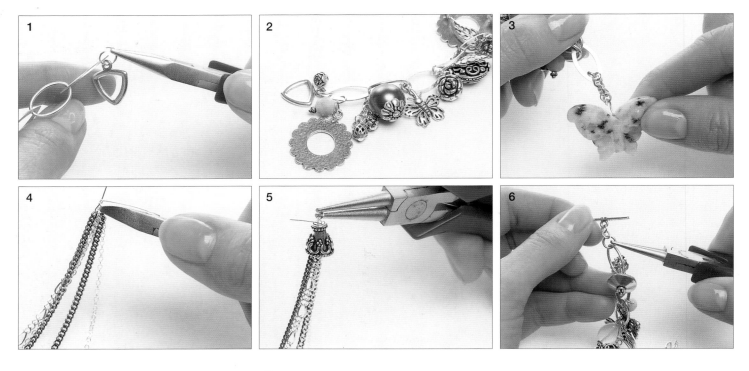

1 Attach the O of the toggle clasp to one end of the chain with an open jump ring.

2 Begin wiring your beads to the chain. Add a bead cap to the large pearl as a decorative touch.

3 To attach the butterfly charm, link the head pin on a small section of chain, which has been looped through the chain bracelet. The butterfly should be about 6 inches into the chain bracelet, as it is the centerpiece of the bracelet.

4 To create a tassel, cut the different silver and gunmetal fine chain into small segments and loop them on the wire.

5 Loop the wire through the bead cone. Wire-wrap this bead cone onto the bracelet chain.

6 Add an open jump ring to the other end of the chain to attach the T-bar of the clasp.

Tips

Wiring each charm to the chain can take time. Before you start your charm bracelet, it is a good idea is to lay your beads out beside the chain to get a feel for how your design will look.

If you are not sure where you want your chain to finish, loop a headpin on to a link of chain, as a reference point, rather than cutting the chain. Beads caps are great if your bead is too big for the headpins, also they hide any imperfections your bead may have.

Variations

You may prefer a less chunky, feminine charm bracelet, such as the one made with pink quartz, metal heart, and fabric beads shown opposite.

Knotted Leather & Turquoise Stone Bracelet

Turquoise is very popular with designers because it's such a fresh and vibrant stone. There is also such variation in the color, shape, and markings of the stone that no two are ever the same. Turquoise is a color description in itself and ranges from pale sky-blue to deep blue-green. Often turquoise stones also have dark swirls or specks in color. The use of turquoise in jewelry dates back several centuries and is common to many cultures. It is found in Arizona and New Mexico, as well as China, Iran, Turkey, and Egypt. It is the official birthstone for the month of December.

I always have a turquoise story in my summer jewelry collections because the refreshing color is perfect for accessorizing a summer wardrobe. The leather strand in this project adds to the natural feel of this beautiful bracelet. I have used a dark silver, Bali-style hook and eye clasp to blend with the streaks of black through the stone and the black leather. You could try brown leather instead, with a gold-color clasp.

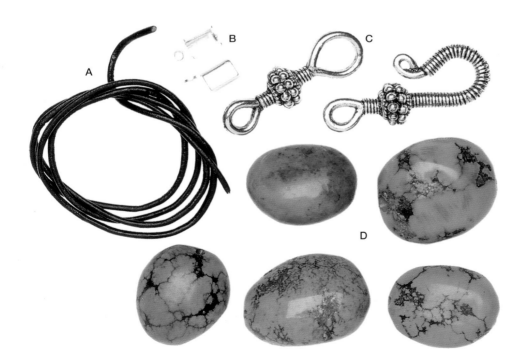

Materials
A Black leather, approx. 1 yard (extra to allow for the knots in the leather)
B Silver leather crimps x 2
C Fancy Bali-style sterling silver hook and eye clasp x 1
D Turquoise nuggets, approx. 9 (this will depend on the size of the stones)

Tools required
Wire cutters
Chain-nose pliers

Techniques
Knotting leather between stones.
Working with leather crimp.

1

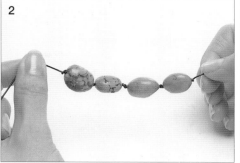

2

3

4

5

Tips

Hook and eye clasps are great clasps to use on a bracelet because they are so easy to close!

When buying any leather or stone make sure the leather will fit through the hole of the bead.

Before cutting any leather, test the length of the knotted bracelet on your wrist first.

1 Loop the leather through a nugget stone.
2 After each nugget, knot the leather tightly. Make sure the stones are close together and the knot is big enough to prevent the stone from slipping over the knot.
3 After your last turquoise nugget stone, add one end of the clasp to the leather.
4 Put the leather crimp over both strands of leather and close firmly with chain-nose pliers. This secures your clasp to the leather.
5 Snip the excess leather with wire cutters.

Semiprecious Garnet Bracelet

This project is a wonderful mix of garnet rondels and metal balls on a gold-filled chain. I bought the stunning garnet rondels, which are matte rather than faceted and sparkly, at a market in Palermo, Sicily, during a vacation, so they are extra-special to me. The matte look of the beads, and the variety of mismatched shapes and imperfections, make them the perfect bead in my view.

Many semiprecious stones are shaped differently, and very often when you buy a strand of stones they will graduate in size from small to larger beads. No two stones on the garnet strand were identical, so the bracelet has a lot of character.

In this project I have used the wire to create my own head pins and made a small decorative loop at the bottom of each pin. Also, you can make a pretty feature by wire-wrapping small garnet stones together at the end of the chain.

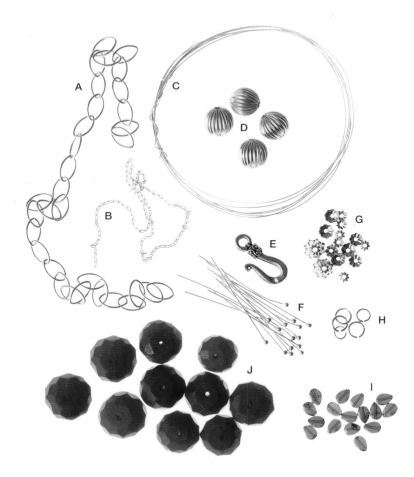

Materials

A Gold-filled oval linked chain, approx. 12 inches
B Gold-filled fine chain, 8 inches
C 24 gauge gold-filled wire
D 10mm gold wavy balls x 4
E Gold-filled fancy hook and eye clasp (in this design, only the hook section of the clasp is used)
F Gold-filled ball pins x 10
G 8mm gold filligree bead caps x 10
H 6mm gold-filled open jump rings x 4
I 12mm semiprecious garnet leaves x 10
J 12mm semiprecious garnet rondels x 10

Tools

Wire cutters
Round-nose pliers
Chain-nose pliers

Techniques

Adding wire-looped beads to the end of chain.
Creating chain tassels on the end of beads.

How to make the semiprecious garnet bracelet

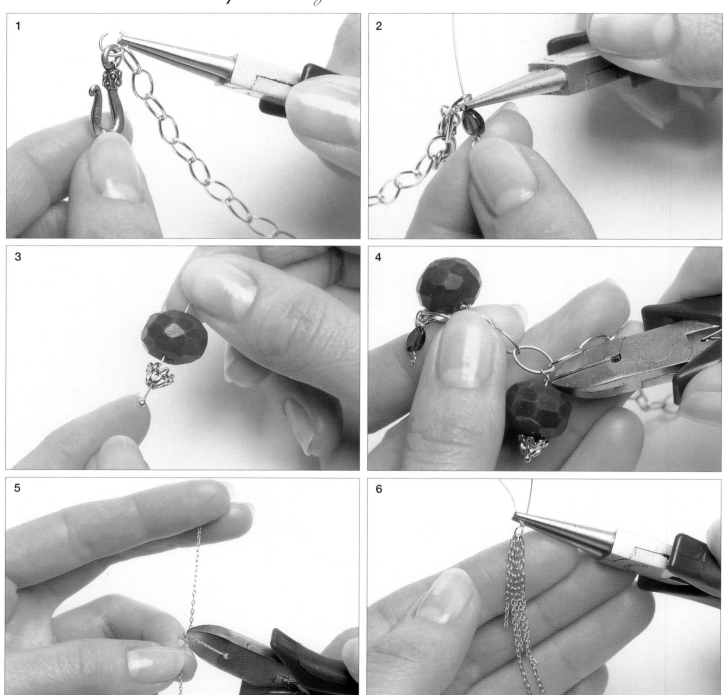

7

Tips

I have not added the eye part of the clasp to this design, as the hook clasp will link through any of the links of the bracelet chain.

Make this bracelet as chunky or delicate as you like!

8

1 Add the hook part of the clasp to one end of chain with a jump ring.

2 Begin wire-wrapping the small garnet beads on to the chain.

3 Add a decorative bead cap and garnet rondel to a ball pin.

4 Wire-wrap the rondel to the chain, and cut any excess wire.

5 To create a tassel, cut the fine chain into even strips of chain.

6 Loop the chain onto about 4 inches of gold-filled wire and wire-wrap a loop (see Key Techniques, page 36).

7 Add a rondel to the wire, and continue to attach to the chain.

8 Keep adding a mix of garnet stones, small garnet leaves and gold balls to your bracelet chain. Add the rosary looped beads to the end of the chain.

Knotted Chain & Crystal Bracelet

What makes jewelry designing so much fun are the infinite combinations you can create with different materials. I found the rhinestone buttons used in this project at my local trimmings store. They are surrounded with Swarovski crystals in different sizes, and what appears as blue/black color crystal in 6mm and 8mm faceted round shapes. The dark gunmetal chain is softened with strands of silver chain.

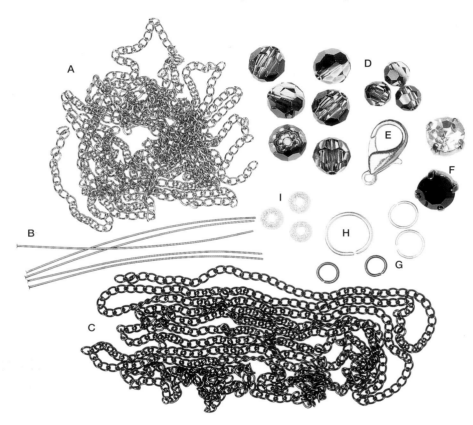

1 Cut about 10 lengths of chain, using a mix of silver and gunmetal chain. Each strip should be about 12 to 14 inches long.
2 Create a neat knot in the 10 strands, 4 inches from the end of the chain. Tie another knot 1¹/₂ to 2 inches away from the first.
3 Add the buttons to the knot using open jump rings. Keep adding crystals to create a beaded knot.
4 Cut a single strand of chain from the knotted chain.
5 Add a 6mm crystal to the cut chain.

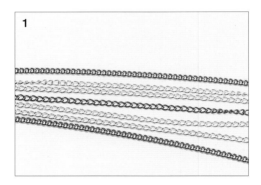

6 Cut all the chain to your desired length for the bracelet.
7 Loop the strands through a large jump ring and attach the clasp to either end.

Tips

This design would look wonderful as a necklace, with one large cluster of crystals and more tassels of chain cascading down with tiny crystals dangling from them.

Materials

A Silver fine chain, approx. 2 yards
B Silver or gunmetal head pins x 15
C Gunmetal fine chain, approx. 2 yards
D A mix of black diamond 6mm and 8mm Swarovski crystals x 10
E 13mm silver lobster clasp x 1
F Crystal sew-on buttons, x 1 silver, 1 jet
G Gunmetal or silver jump rings x 7
H Large silver open jump ring
I 6mm silver stardust metal balls x 3

Tools

Wire cutters
Round-nose; chain-nose pliers

Techniques

Cutting and knotting chain.
Creating tassels.
Adding buttons using jump rings.

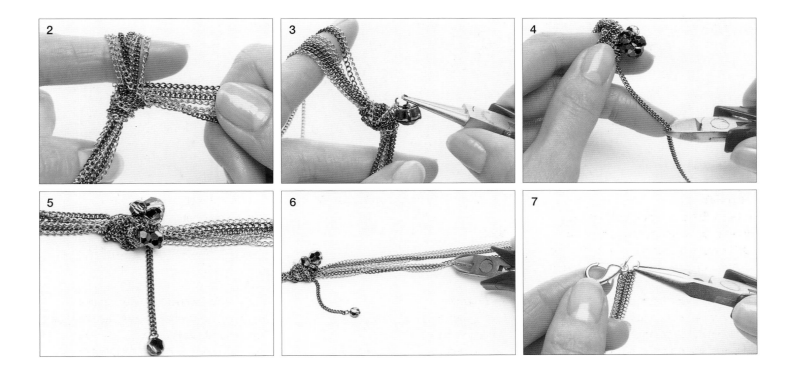

Wired Crystal, Suede & Chain Bracelet

This project is very unusual; each strand of this striking bracelet is interesting. It uses a mix of chains, including pretty filigree chain, suede, and a rhinestone strand, and chunky, wired crystal stones. The latter are quite light in weight, so I could have added a complete strand of crystals wire-looped together, but I think the combination of chain and crystals is very effective and keeps the design from being too bulky. And, of course, the strip of rhinestone adds sparkle.

Materials

A & B 3 different styles of chunky gold-plated chain, approx. 12 inches each
C Fancy oval filigree gold-plated chain, approx. 12 inches
D Gold toggle clasp x 1
E Large crystal stones x 3
F Gold diamanté strand, approx. 12 inches
G 26 or 28 gauge gold wire
H 6mm gold jump rings x 4
I Brown suede, approx. 16 inches

Tools

Wire cutters
Round-nose pliers
Chain-nose pliers
Scissors
Superglue

Techniques

Threading suede through chain.
Wire-wrapping stones to chain.
Adding wire around a bead to add a feature.

Tips

When selecting the suede, make sure it will thread through the chain links. Likewise, make sure your wire will fit through the crystal stones you use.

Sometimes toggle clasps are difficult to close so you may need to add two or three jump rings to the T-bar of the clasp.

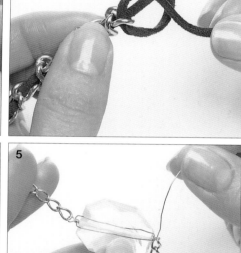

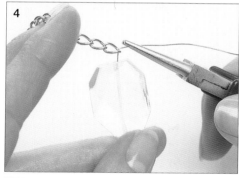

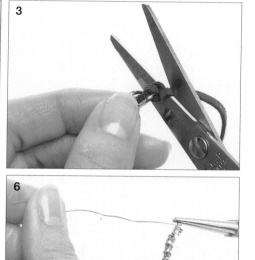

1 Thread the suede through the thickest chain.

2 Knot the suede on the last link of chain.

3 Cut the suede and add a dab of superglue to keep it in place. Repeat steps 2 and 3 on the other end of the chain.

4 Wire-wrap the crystals to the next strip of chain, which should be finer.

5 Add extra gold wire around the crystals, to make a feature of them.

6 Create a wire-wrap loop on the rhinestone strand.

7 Join all the different strands of chain and the rhinestone strand together using an open jump ring to the O-part of the clasp. Do the same at the other end using an open jump ring and the T-bar of the clasp.

Chain & Crystal Disk Bracelet

This gorgeous bracelet consists of a mix of strands of chain with reflective sew-on Swarovski crystals. This mix makes it seem like several different bracelets all looped together, and the wire-wrapped faceted briolettes add a delicate touch to the heavy chain, as well as a different shape. It is one of my favorite bracelets – the golden brown color goes with absolutely everything – and I always get compliments when I wear it.

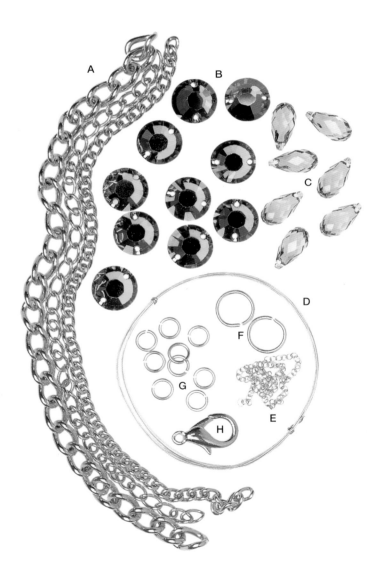

Materials

A 3 different types of gold cable chain, 8 inches
B Sew-on round Swarovski crystals x 13
C 5.5mm Swarovski crystal faceted drop/briolettes x 11
D 28 gauge/ 0.4mm gold-filled wire
E Fine, 1.4mm cable chain, 12 inches
F 12mm gold open jump rings x 2
G 6mm gold open jump rings x 16
H 13mm gold lobster clasp

Tools

Wire cutters
Round-nose pliers
Chain-nose pliers

Techniques

Cutting chain.
Wire-wrapping crystal briolettes.

How to make the chain & crystal disk bracelet

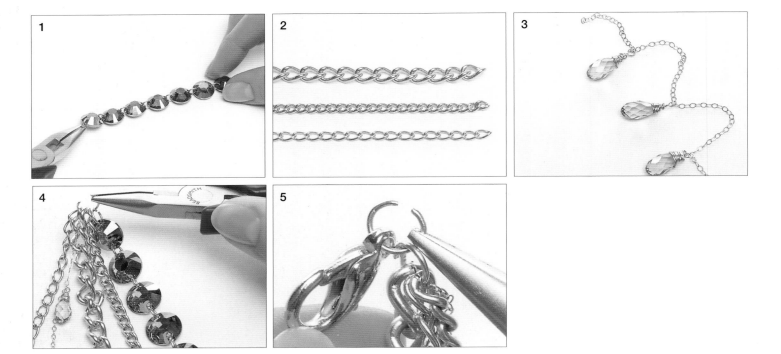

1 Join each of the 13 disks together with open jump rings.

2 Ensure the three types of chain are cut to the same length, about 7¹/₂ inches.

3 Wire-wrap the briolette crystals to the fine chain, see Key Techniques (page 39).

4 Join the chains together onto an open jump ring, and the links of sew-on crystals to the open jump ring, and close firmly.

5 Add the clasp with an open jump ring and close firmly to secure. Repeat at the other end with another jump ring.

Tips

I often use an extra large lobster clasp on bracelets, as well as an extender chain at the other end, which makes it easier to put the bracelet on.

Remember to be patient when wire-wrapping; it can be very difficult with delicate crystal briolettes, so practice on base metal wire first.

Variations

The crystal disks come in a variety of hues, so experiment with different colors. Opposite, purple stones have been paired with amethyst quartz teardrops, which makes a stunning combination.

Antique Pearl Bracelet

Vintage-style bracelets are always special. To give this pearl and gunmetal chain design just such a feel, I have added a filigree box clasp. To keep it sparkly, and liven up the chain and dark-colored beads, I have used oval labradorite gemstones, which are a grayish, almost opaque, form of mineral with flashes of blue, green, and/or yellow visible at certain angles. The gemstone's iridescent color is matched with the AB-coated 4mm Swarovski bicone crystals, which are very reflective and sparkly.

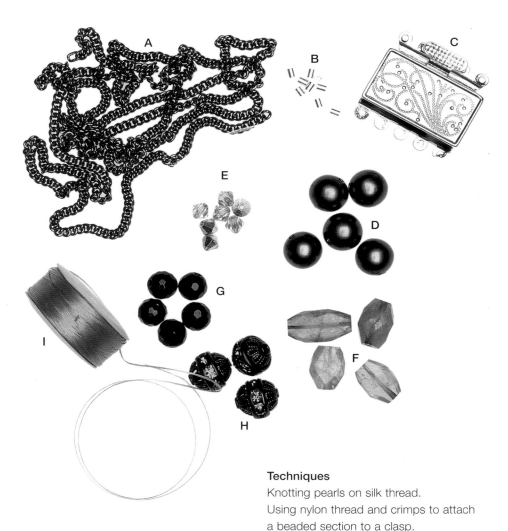

Materials

A Fine gunmetal chain, 12 inches
B Gunmetal or silver crimps x 4
C 5-strand antique-style box clasp
D 8mm gray glass pearls x 17
E 4mm bicone vitrail medium Swarovski crystals x 15
F Faceted labradorite oval stones x 15
G 6mm faceted round onyx beads x 30
H 8mm rhinestone metal ball with green crystals
I Grey silk thread, approx. 24 inches
Also:
Nylon monofilament (nylon fishing line), approx. 12 inches
28 gauge/0.4mm gunmetal wire
6mm jump rings x 4
Gunmetal bead tips x 2

Tools

Wire cutters
Round-nose pliers
Chain-nose pliers
Needle

Tips

It can sometimes be difficult to locate interesting gunmetal chains, so if you find a silver chain that you like, but you want it in a gunmetal color, it can easily be dyed using an oxidized solution available at craft stores.

Techniques

Knotting pearls on silk thread.
Using nylon thread and crimps to attach a beaded section to a clasp.

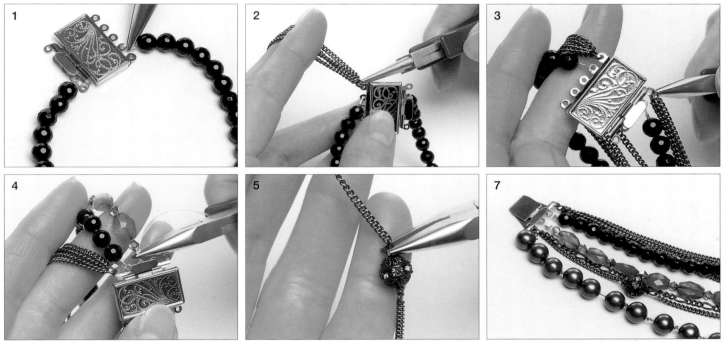

1 Thread the onyx beads through the nylon monofilament and then attach to the second ring of the clasp using a crimp bead, looping the nylon through the ring of the clasp and back through the crimp.

2 Attach three strands of gunmetal chain with an open jump ring to the first ring of the clasp.

3 Repeat this on the other end of the clasp.

4 Add the strand of labradorite and crystals to the third ring of the clasp, securing with a crimp bead.

5 Wire-wrap the rhinestone balls on the fine gunmetal chain, then add to the fourth ring of the clasp.

6 Add the pearl knotted strand to the last ring. (See pearl knotting on page 112.)

Earrings

Earrings

Earrings are the ultimate fashion accessory. They are my favorite type of jewelry, and if I am going out in the evening, I love to don a pair of colorful, sparkly chandelier earrings that really make a statement. Like most jewelry, they are a very personal choice. Often people have a favorite pair that with go with many outfits. I hope one of the following projects will become your favorite pair.

We start by creating a classic pair of white baroque pearl drop earrings, then move onto fabulous clustered gemstone earrings, sparkly hoops, and chandeliers using memory wire and chandelier components. All the projects provide invaluable techniques in creating your own pair of stunning earrings.

Variations
This variation on the classic Pearl Drop Earrings (page 76) uses several pearls instead of just one. Odd-numbered combinations usually work best, so try either three or five pearls together, which can graduate in size also.

Pearl Drop Earrings

Pearls are timeless and classic; a pair of pearl drops are often a staple part of a jewelry box. Although some people feel pearls are outdated, they are truly feminine and will match most outfits. Here I have created a pair of beautiful pearl drops using lush cream baroque pearls wire-wrapped together. The simplicity of the design, which focuses on highlighting the beautiful colors and textures of the pearls, makes them a great starter project.

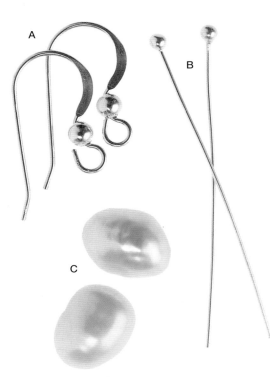

Materials
A Fish-hooks x 2
B Fine-gauge ball head pins
C Baroque-shaped freshwater pearls x 2

Tools
Wire cutters
Round-nose pliers
Chain-nose pliers

Techniques
Wire-wrapping pearls.

1 Place a head pin through the pearl.
2 Bend the wire at a 90 degree angle.
3 Use round-nose pliers to make a loop at the top of the bead.
4 Snip the excess wire with cutters.
5 Open the ring of the earring hook and loop the pearl onto the ring.
6 Close the ring of the earring securely with the chain-nose pliers. Repeat to create a matching pair.

Tips
Make sure the pearls are drilled right through so that you can insert a head pin.

   In this example the earrings are wire-looped, but you could also rosary loop the pearls. Make sure, though, that the loops are firmly closed when rosary looping, so they are secure.

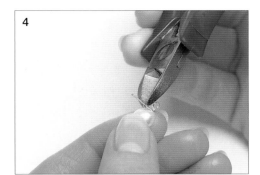

4

5

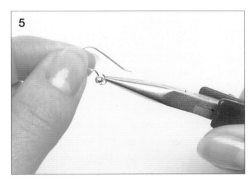

6

Variations

You may like to add some color to the baroque pearls using tiny 3mm bicone crystals on silver wire. Alternatively, you could embellish the design with more small crystals or rice pearls.

Turquoise Hoop Earrings

Hoops are amazing, and the most fantastic component to work with since there are so many wonderful combinations you can create. They come in a variety of size and styles, from small to large and plain metal to swirl metal. I definitely recommend creating your very own pair of hooped gems. Here I have created a classic pair of hoop earrings with turquoise teardrops, mixed with fabulous shaped crystals, on sterling silver hoops.

Materials

A Turquoise teardrops x 2
B Fine sterling silver chain, approx. 6 inches
C A mix of 6mm AB, bicone, rondel, and flower-shaped crystals (margarites)
D Blue drop-shaped crystals x 2
E 0.4mm/28–30 gauge sterling silver wire
F Sterling silver hoops x 2
G Silver ball head pins x 12

Tools

Cutters
Round-nose pliers
Chain-nose pliers

Techniques

Wire-wrapping teardrops.
Adding crystals to fine chain.
Looping chain through earring hoops.

How to make the turquoise hoop earrings

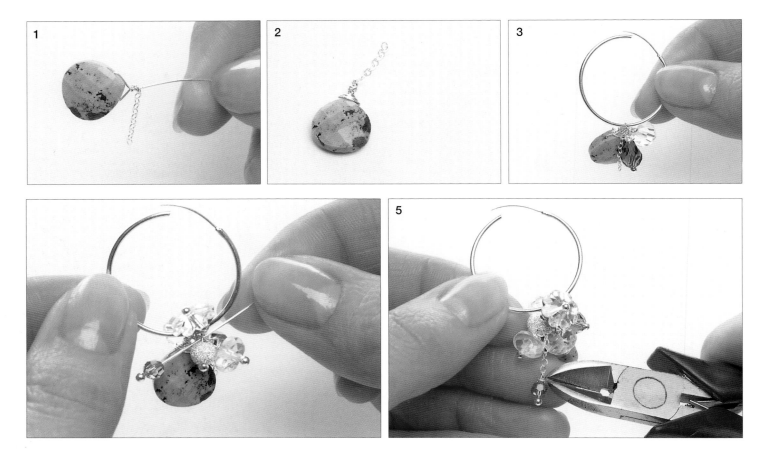

1 Wire-wrap the turquoise stone onto the last link of chain. See Key Techniques (page 39).

2 Make sure the wire is neatly coiled.

3 Loop through the silver earring hoop. Wire-wrap the crystals onto the fine wire with the head pins. Add your cluster of crystals to the hoop.

4 Keep adding more crystals to the cluster.

5 Snip any excess wire on the crystals.

Tips

Use smaller hoops if you prefer, or make the chain longer and add bigger beads for a chunky statement look.

Variations

See opposite for a pair of gold hoops with carnelian (a form of quartz), dusty balls and gold bicones.

For delicate daywear, use 12–20mm hoops; if you want to go for something big, use 30–50mm hoops.

Crystal Clip-On Earrings

Many vintage earrings are clip-ons, and although they can be difficult to find these days, they are certainly coming back into fashion. The peach-colored crystals used here make for a fabulous statement pair of clip-on earrings.

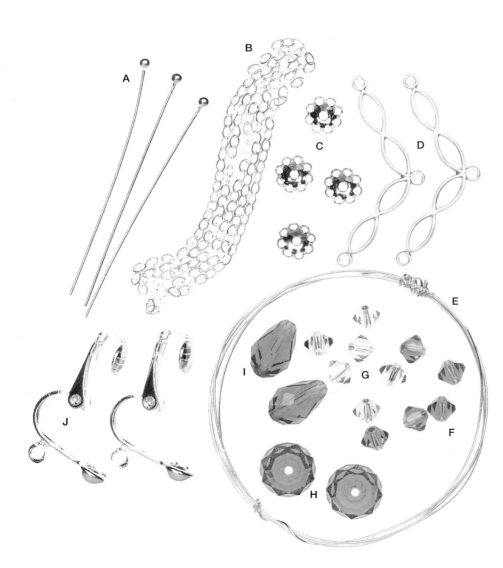

Materials

A Silver ball pins x 6
B Silver fine chain, approx. 24 inches
C Silver bead caps
D Silver oval components x 2
E Silver wire, approx. 12 inches
F 4mm padparadscha bicone crystals x 2
H 6mm padparadscha crystal rondels x 2
F 4mm padparadscha bicone crystals x 2
G 4mm crystal silver colored bicone crystals x 2
H 6mm padparadscha crystal rondels x 2
I 9 x 6mm padparadscha faceted drops x 4
J Silver clip-on earrings

Tools

Wire cutters
Round-nose pliers
Chain-nose pliers

Techniques

Wire-wrapping components to crystals.
Adding chain to metal components.

How to make the crystal clip-on earrings

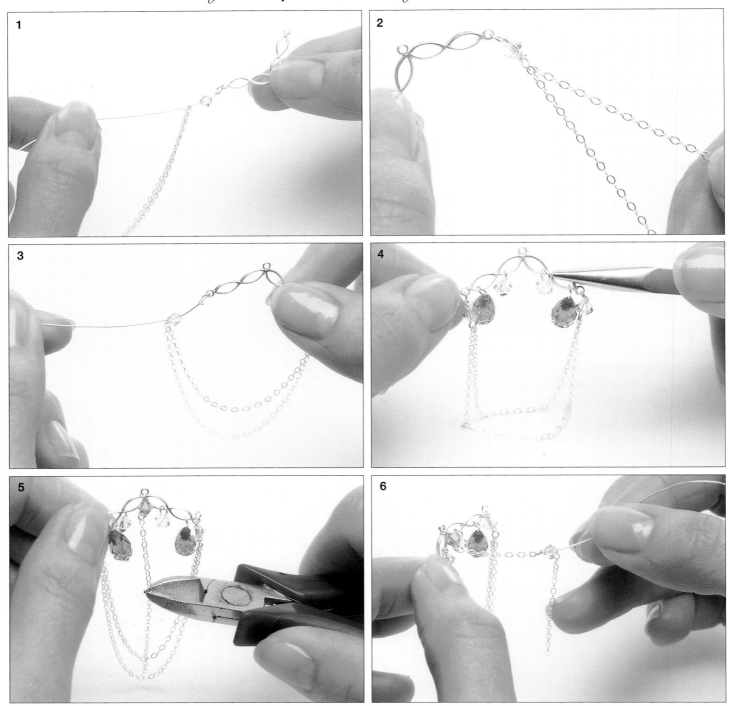

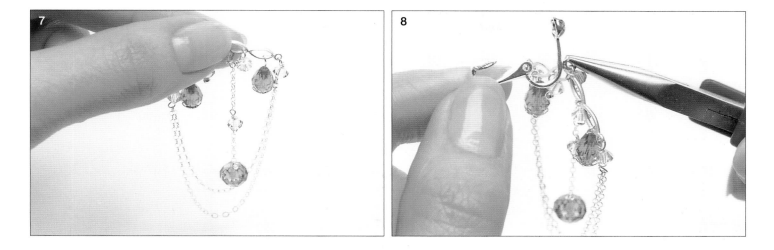

1 & 2 Wire-wrap one 4mm silver bicone to the metal component. Wire-wrap the other end of the crystal to two strands of fine chain.

3 Repeat this on the other side of the component.

4 Add a padparadscha faceted drop and a 4mm silver bicone crystal to the two decorative loops on each side of the component.

5 On the center loop of the component, add a 4mm padparadscha crystal bicone and chain. Cut the chain at about 1½ inches.

6 Wire-wrap a 4mm crystal to the center piece of chain.

7 Add the padparadscha rondel to the last link of chain, to complete your center feature.

8 Loop your beaded component through the loop of the clip-on earring hoops. Repeat to create the matching earring.

Tips

The small silver components give these earrings structure and form. You could also use them in necklace designs.

Variations

For those who do not have pierced ears, there are many clip-on converters available, which allow you to convert post earrings to clip-ons. The post of a pierced earring simply slides directly into the cylinder of the clip-on earring.

Phrenite Oval Chandelier Earrings

What is so captivating about this design are the beautiful stones within the stylish oval gold-filled component. They swing inside the metal oval, giving the design an intriguing three-dimensional structure. In this design you can see the use of complementary tones, in this case varying shades of green, which work wonderfully together. I use light Colorado topaz crystal stones frequently in my designs because their soft color blends well with other shade: they are perfect accent beads for earrings.

In assembling this chandelier jewelry, I've used only two links of gold-filled oval-shaped chain. This is a great example of why you should never throw away any chain you love – even if it's only one link! – as you will always find a use for it. Also, a subtle, but effective, part of the symmetry of the earrings is that the chain's oval links mirror the oval-shaped component, on a smaller scale.

Materials

A 0.4mm gauge gold-filled wire or gold-filled ball head pins x 10
B 4mm and 6mm blue zircon bicone Swarovski crystals, 2 of each
C 4mm light Colorado topaz bicone Swarovski crystals x 2
D 7 x 9 mm faceted oval, side-drilled apatite stones x 2
E Large phrenite stone x 2
F Gold-filled earring posts x 2
G 6mm gold stardust metal ball x 2
H 21 x 47mm gold-filled oval components, x 2
I Oval-shaped chain links, approx. 2 links

Tools

Wire cutters
Chain-nose pliers
Round-nose pliers

Techniques

Using chandelier components.
Wire-wrapping chain and beads together.

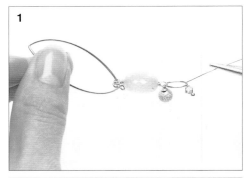

1

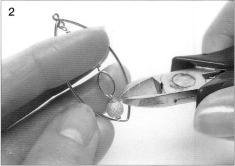

2

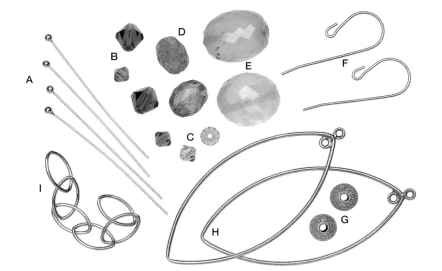

1 Wire-wrap one end of the phrenite semiprecious stone to the chandelier component and the other end to one link of chain. Begin to add other beads, including the stardust metal ball.

2 Wire-wrap the beads using ball head pins. Snip excess wire with wire cutters.

3 Add the apatite beads and remaining Swarovski crystals.

4 Attach to the open ring of the earring hoop. Close the earring hoop firmly with chain-nose pliers to secure. Repeat to create a matching pair.

Tips

Some semiprecious stones can be brittle, so treat them carefully. It is also important, when using semiprecious stones in your earring designs, to make sure the stones are not too heavy to wear. It's also best to choose stones that are of a similar size and shape.

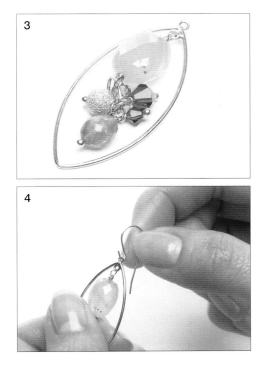

Jet Crystal & Chain Chandelier Earrings

These sophisticated but very wearable earrings are made particularly striking by the use of jet colored beads. The design demonstrates how fantastic memory wire is for creating this type of earring.

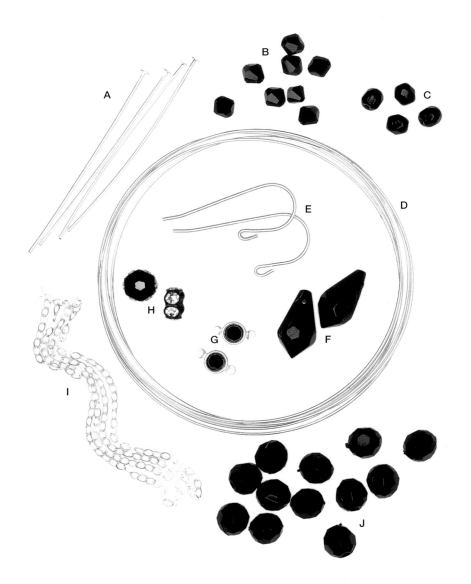

Materials

A Silver head pins x 6
B 4mm jet bicone crystals x 14
C Jet glass 4mm bead x 4
D Bracelet-size memory wire x 3 coils
E Silver earring hooks x 2
F Jet crystal teardrops x 2
G Jet disks x 2
H Jet rhinestone rondels x 8
I Silver fine chain, approx. 16 inches
J 6mm jet round glass beads x 20

Tools

Wire cutters
Memory-wire cutters
Heavy-duty round-nose pliers
Chain-nose pliers

Techniques

Working with memory wire to create chandelier components.

How to make the jet crystal and chain chandelier earrings

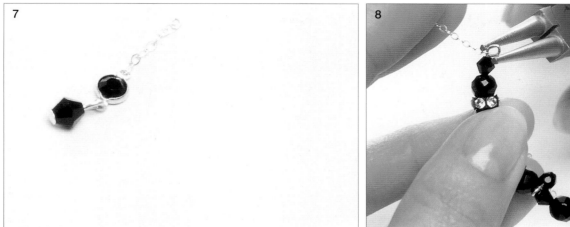

7

8

1 Cut the memory wire into a semicircle and curl it around one end of the wire round using sturdy round-nose pliers.

2 Start to add your beads to the memory wire, in the following order: 4mm crystal, 6mm glass bead, rhinestone rondel, 6mm glass bead.

3 Add fine chain to the memory wire.

4 Keep adding beads, following the pattern.

5 Add a 4mm glass bead to a head pin and create a rosary loop at the top of the head pin, to loop onto the memory wire.

6 Add the crystal teardrop; this is the center of your memory wire loop. Then loop the other end of chain from step 3 onto the memory wire. (The length of the chain in this design is 3 inches, though it can vary.) Keep adding your beads.

7 Take a few links of chain and add a jet disk and a 4mm crystal to the bottom.

8 Add a 1 1/4 -inch strip of chain to the curled end of the memory wire. Repeat on the other end of the memory wire. Loop the two strips of chain from the other end of the memory wire, and the small chain

drop from step 7 through the earring hook. Close the earring hook firmly. Repeat to create the matching earring.

Tips

Use the same position on the round-nose pliers to re-create same-shaped loops.

Variations

Creating your own chandelier components with memory wire is great fun and gives you a lot of flexibility. The size of the memory wire semicircle will determine the size of your earrings, so you can make them smaller. The variation shown on page 5 uses a lot more chain with three-tiered chain loops. This design is a mix of amazonite teardrops and Pacific opal crystals with gold metal findings.

Small Briolette Teardrop Chain Earrings

There are several possibilies when creating clustered chain earrings – you can add clusters of gems randomly to the chain or you can wire-wrap all the chain, as has been done in this project. The two complementing peridot and tourmaline gems came from eBay, and I think the two colors work beautifully together. This is a great project for practicing a very important skill, delicate wire-wrapping.

Materials

A Sterling silver earring hooks x 2
B 28–30 gauge/0.4mm sterling silver wire
C Pink peridot gem teardrops x 12
D Tourmaline gem teardrops x 12
E Fine sterling silver cable chain, approx. 3 inches

Tools

Cutters
Round-nose pliers
Chain-nose pliers

Techniques

Wire-wrapping delicate gems to fine chain.

1 Wire-wrap one teardrop to the end of the chain. See Key Techniques (page 39). Make sure the wire is neatly coiled around the gem.

2 Continue add teardrops to the chain. Open the ring of the earring and loop the chain through, then close the loop firmly. Repeat to create the matching pair.

Tips

Remember to practice on plated wire before working with sterling silver or gold-filled wire, and don't rush it! It will take time to master.

With such small gems you may prefer to use miniature round-nose pliers.

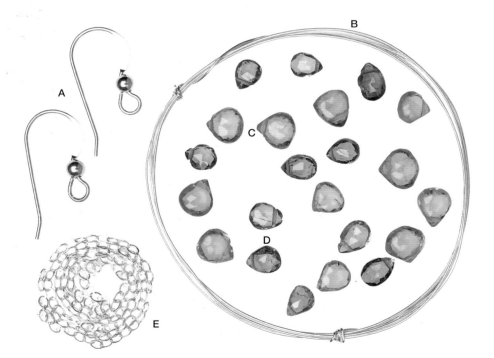

Classic Garnet Hoops

Finding the perfect hooped earrings can be difficult, so why not make your own stunning pair? For this project I have used a mixture of garnet stones that I have had for some time and have been saving for a special occasion. Unlike the matte garnet rondels used in the bracelet project, these red stones are shiny and glossy.

Materials

A 7mm oval garnet beads x 12
B 6mm round garnet beads x 12
C 4mm rondel garnet beads x 12
D 4mm round light Colorado topaz crystals x 8
E 4mm light Colorado topaz bicone crystals x 8
F Gold hoops x 2
G Gold crimp beads x 4
H Gold-filled ball pins x 52

Tools

Wire cutters
Round-nose pliers
Chain-nose pliers
Crimp pliers

Techniques

Using crimp beads on components.
Working with hoops.

1 Create a wired stone on a ball pin (see Key Techniques, page 39).

2 Add a crimp bead to your hoops. Start adding the wired stones, mixing the shapes and sizes of the beads.

3 Once you are happy with the cluster, press down on the crimp beads with chain-nose pliers or crimp pliers. This will keep the cluster of gems centered on the hoop.

4 Using chain-nose pliers, lift the top of the hoop so that it fits into the round end of the other end of the loop. Repeat to create a matching pair.

Tips

Ball pins add a decorative finish to the end of the bead.

Filigree Chandelier Earrings

The ethnic-inspired filigree chandelier component in oxidized sterling silver used in this project has five loops on which I've hung a mixture of crystal bicones and round crystals with delicate rice pearls, the latter giving a lovely delicate finish to the earrings. Chandelier components in sterling silver or gold-filled wire are a great foundation to making chandelier earrings.

Materials

A Sterling silver fish hook earrings
B 0.4mm/28–30 gauge sterling silver wire
C 3mm rice pearls x 12
D 19mm oxidized sterling silver filigree, 5-looped chandeliers x 2
E 6mm black diamond crystal bicones x 8
F 6mm AB crystal rounds x 10
G 4mm AB black diamond crystal bicones x 6

Tools

Wire cutters
Round-nose pliers
Chain-nose pliers

Techniques

Attaching wire-wrapped loops to chandelier components.
Working with delicate crystals and pearls.

How to make the filigree chandelier earrings

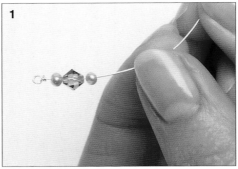

the loops of the chandelier.
7 Loop the top through the earring hoop.
Repeat to create a matching pair.

The pattern on the chandelier loops is:
Loops 1 and 5:
6mm round, rice pearl, 4mm crystal
Loops 2 and 4:
6mm bicone, 6mm round, rice pearl
Loop 3:
4mm bicone, 6mm bicone, 6mm round,
rice pearl

Tips

Wire-wrapping takes time, so before you
begin, lay out your crystals and pearls on a
bead mat to get a feel for the design.
Remember that where you place your wire
on the barrel of the round-nose pliers will
determine the size of the loop.

1 Add a pearl, a 6mm crystal, and then
another pearl to your wire.
2 Attach the beaded wire to the top of the
chandelier component.
3 Wire-wrap your next section of pearl,
6mm crystal and 4mm crystal.
4 Join the sections together.
5 Wire-wrap the top crystal to the
chandelier loop.
6 Keep adding the wire-wrap sections to

Variations

*The pair on the right are what I call my
"Beyonce" earrings – they are so big you
won't be missed when wearing them! You
don't need to go this big, obviously, but I
loved making them, and everyone
comments on how fabulous they look. The
gold metal component is a large, 8-hole
vermeil chandelier, to which I have wire-
wrapped odd–shaped amethyst stones
with tiny sapphire rondels, and a mix of
4mm and 6mm purple bicones and round
crystals. The beautiful faceted semiprecious
stones are amazing.*

Necklaces

Necklaces

When you begin designing jewelry, it is easy to be overwhelmed by the choice and variety of what you can make. With such a vast range of beautiful materials to work with, it is often very difficult to get started. I hope, though, that the following eight projects – which include a timeless, knotted pearl multistrand necklace, a turquoise leather pendant necklace that is perfect for summer, an evening must-have of clustered crystals on chain, and a long, beaded statement tassel necklace – will provide you with the inspiration to create your own beautiful designs.

The selection of designs vary in complexity and techniques. Many of them also use a variety of components, including chain, leather, ribbon, crystals, acrylic, pearls, and semiprecious stones. Necklaces are now so much a part of everyday attire that they are one of the first things we add to liven up our wardrobe.

Variations
If the gunmetal and golden tones on page 104 are too strong for you, the feminine design opposite, where the pretty pink crystal teardrop is complemented with hot pink crystals, may appeal.

Teardrop Pendant Necklace

Pendant necklaces are a fabulous, stylish addition to any jewelry box, and wearing several together creates a particularly distinctive, individual look. Using chunkier chain and beads will create a statement piece of jewelry that really stands out, whereas using thinner chain and beads will give you a more delicate design.

In this glamorous design I have used a cluster of sparkly, faceted Swarovski crystals in a variety of amazing shapes – large teardrop, baroque, round – on gunmetal chain. I have also mixed golden and black tones together, for a striking effect, and used two different types of chain – fine and figaro style.

Materials

A 38 x 22mm golden teak, Swarovski strass teardrops

B A mix of Swarovski crystals – drop pendant, 8mm and 14mm faceted round and baroque-style, jet-colored crystals, large oval and round-shaped crystals in crystal and crystal AB

C Gold or gunmetal head pins

D Open jump rings x 4

E 11mm gunmetal lobster clasp

F Gold bead tips x 3

G Gold or gunmetal bails x 2

H Gunmetal fine cable link chain, approx. 24 inches

I Gunmetal figaro link, approx. 24 inches

Tools

Wire cutters
Round-nose pliers
Chain-nose pliers

Techniques

Creating a cluster with crystals.

Tips

Experiment with necklace lengths before cutting the chain. Or add an extender chain so you can adjust the length.

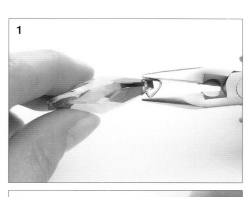

1

2

3

1 Add a bail to the teardrop, then close it firmly with chain-nose pliers.

2 Create a cluster of crystals of different shapes. Join the cluster of crystals and teardrop onto one jump ring. Close the jump ring firmly with chain-nose pliers. Attach this cluster to a large jump ring.

3 Loop the large jump ring through the two types of gunmetal chain. Finish by attaching a clasp and jump ring to each end of the chain.

Wire-Looped Pearl Necklace

Pearls are incredibly pretty beads to work with and they have a timeless appeal. This beautiful piece of jewelry, with its random mix of mother-of-pearl and baroque pearls attached to a medium-sized circle link chain, is a modern take on the classic pearl necklace. It is the perfect design for reworking a strand of pearls you may not wear any more. I firmly believe that you should never throw away any jewelry, as you can always rework it into something lovely.

Materials

A Large gold-filled circle chain, approx. 8 inches
B Rectangular mother-of-pearl beads x 8
C 8mm baroque pearls x 12
D Mother-of-pearl chips x 10
E Oval mother-of-pearl beads x 8
F 28 gauge/0.4mm gold-filled wire

Tools

Wire cutters
Round-nose pliers
Chain-nose pliers

Techniques

Wire-wrapping pearls to chain.
Looping beads together.

1 Wire-wrap a mother-of-pearl oval bead to the large link chain.
2 Snip any excess wire.
3 Using wire cutters, cut four links of chain.
4 Continue wrapping and adding pearls and shells until you have your desired length.

Tips

You don't need to add a clasp to this necklace as, at 36 inches, the length is quite long and will easily go over your head. You could even make it longer, into an opera-style necklace, so that you could wrap it round twice.

When wire-wrapping the pearls together, make sure you loop onto the wire of the other wrapped bead to join them together (see Key Techniques, page 39).

This design would make a perfect matching set with the three-strand Stretch Bracelet with Ribbon (shown on page 1). Just add a ribbon bow to this necklace.

A

B

C

D

E

F

Ribbon, Chain & Mother-of-Pearl Flower Necklace

The emphasis in this classic yet fasionable necklace is on the carved mother-of-pearl flower pendant, which works wonderfully with the wired faceted quartz teardrops and ribbon chain. You could add more teardrops, or larger ones, for even more impact. The black ribbon gives the necklace a softer touch. As an alternative, you could try threading different colored or patterned ribbon, or use leather.

Mother-of-pearl is very popular with jewelry designers because of its lustrous shimmer. The colors can range from off-white, through yellow or golden colors, to even a pinkish, light gray tone.

Materials

A Silver cable chain in two different sizes, approx. 18 inches
B 28 gauge/0.4mm silver wire
C Open jump rings x 3
D 6cm black ribbon, approx. 1½ yards
E 8 x 6mm clear quartz and jet teardrops
F Large carved mother-of-pearl flower x 1

Tools

Wire cutters
Round-nose pliers
Chain-nose pliers

Techniques

Wire-wrapping teardrops to chain.
Looping ribbon through chain.
Attaching large pendants to chain.

How to make the ribbon, chain & mother-of-pearl necklace

1 Cut the ribbon end at an angle.

2 Loop the ribbon through the larger link chain.

3 Knot the ribbon to the last link of chain. You can add a touch of superglue to keep it in place. Cut the ribbon, leaving about 8 inches at each end. Repeat at the other end of the chain. The extra ribbon at either end works as your tie-up clasp.

4 Add the finer link chain to the larger link chain using an open jump ring.

5 Approximately 5 inches from the end of the chain, attach the flower pendant with an open jump ring.

6 Wire-wrap the quartz teardrops to the finer chain, about 2 inches apart, alternating between black and clear teardrops.

7 Join the two types of chain together at the other end with an open jump ring.

Tips

To prevent the cut ribbon from fraying, carefully heat-seal the ends by placing over a flame.

Variations

This take on the ribbon and chain necklace (opposite) has a faux-leather flower instead of the mother-of-pearl flower, plus I have looped leather instead of ribbon through the large link chain. I won the faux-leather flower brooch on an eBay auction, and it makes a wonderful feature to the necklace. I removed the clip part on the back of the brooch and wire-wrapped it to a link of the chain. Another difference is the use of the jet acrylic beads in odd shapes.

Three-Strand Knotted Pearl Necklace

A strand of pearls is a timeless piece of jewelry that is always stylish – think of the style icons Audrey Hepburn and Jackie O. Today there is a fabulous choice of glass pearl beads, in a range of wonderful colors, so don't limit yourself to only traditional white or cream. For this modern twist on the classic three-strand knotted pearl necklace, I have used bronze Swarovski glass pearls, which are incredibly rich in color and have a beautiful, subtle sheen to them, plus a gold, vintage-style, fan-shaped clasp.

Materials
A Chocolate-brown silk thread, 1 spool
B 6mm Swarovski pearls x 100
C 8mm Swarovski pearls x 24
D 10mm Swarovski pearls x 24
E Gold color bead tips x 6
F Gold, 3-row, fan-shaped clasp x 1

Tools
Scissors
Needle
Chain-nose pliers

Techniques
Knotting pearls on silk thread.
Attaching thread to a clasp using bead tips.

Tips
Silk thread is the best thread to use when threading pearls as it allows them to drape better.

How to make the three-strand knotted pearl necklace

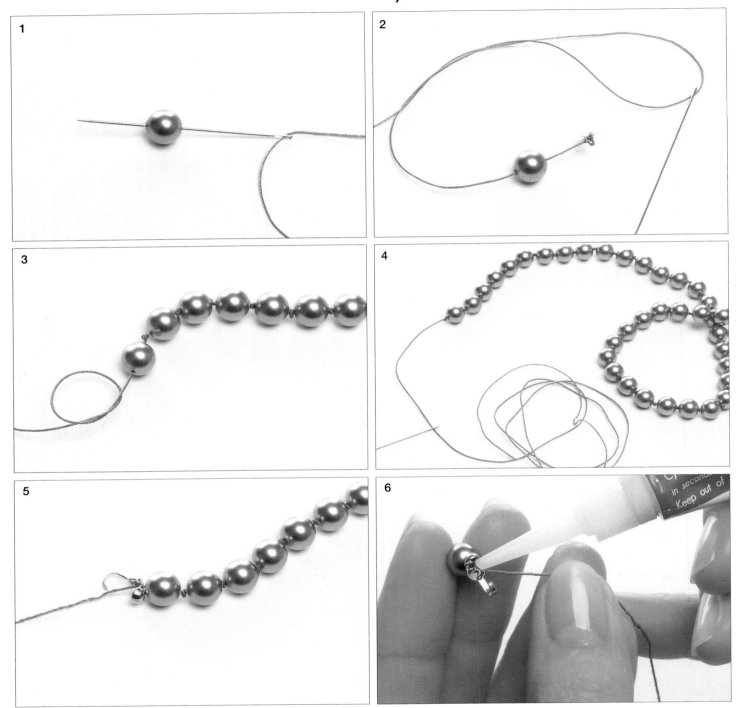

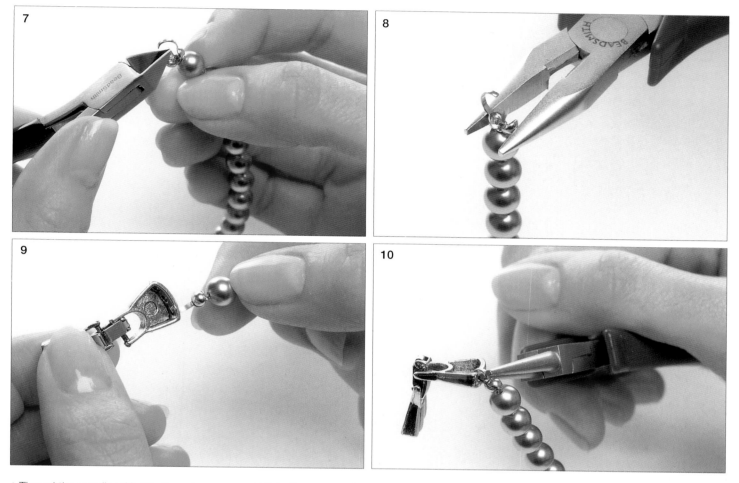

1 Thread the needle with silk thread.

2 Begin the first strand of the necklace by threading the needle through a 6mm pearl.

3 After each pearl, tie a double knot to secure it. Make sure the knot is big enough to prevent the pearl from slipping over it.

4 Continue to thread the 6mm pearls onto the silk thread.

5. After the last pearl and knot, add a bead cap to the thread. Create a double knot after the bead tip.

6 Add a dab of superglue to the knot, and let it dry.

7 Snip the excess thread with cutters or scissors.

8 Press the two shell sides of the bead tip firmly together with chain-nose pliers.

9 Loop open the ring part at the top of the bead tip and attach it to the first row of the clasp.

10 Use chain-nose pliers to close the ring. The first strand is now attached to the clasp. Repeat the process for the second and third strands of pearls, attaching the thread to the clasp with bead tips.

Strand 1: 6mm pearls x 51
Strand 2: 6mm pearls x 24
    8mm pearls x 24
Strand 3: 6mm pearls x 25
    10mm pearls x 24

Turquoise Leather Pendant

Leather and suede strands are often used to make thong-style necklaces, and there is a wide range of faux leather and suede available in many different colors. A popular design is to dangle charms and beads from a closed ring attached to a leather thong. For this eye-catching necklace I have used a slightly coarse leather strand and added a very large oval-shaped turquoise stone that I have mixed with gold metal charms and carved flower-bud turquoise stones. A leather and turquoise necklace like this is fabulous for summer days as it the perfect accessory to a simple white T-shirt or summer dress.

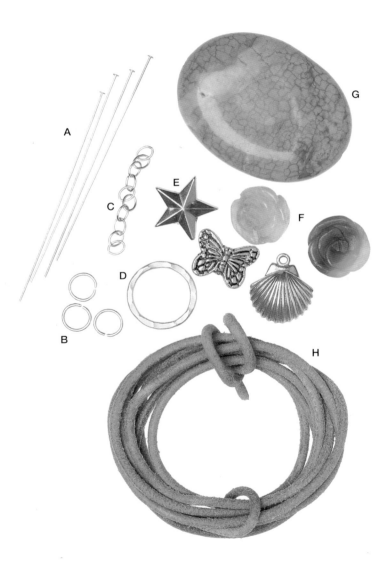

Materials

A Gold pins x 4
B Open jump rings x 4
C Fine gold chain, approx. 2 inches
D Large closed jump ring x 1
E Gold charm beads x 3
F Carved flower-bud turquoise stones (try to select different colored stones) x 2
G 50mm turquoise stone x 1

Tools

Wire cutters
Round-nose pliers
Chain-nose pliers

Techniques

Adding tassels to beads.
Adding large pendant stones to leather.
Creating an adjustable knot finish.

Variations

The variation shown on page 2 is a beautifully detailed cloisonné bead on a strand of brown suede. This fabulous 39 x 10mm enameled flower disk necklace is simple but stunning.

How to make the turquoise leather pendant

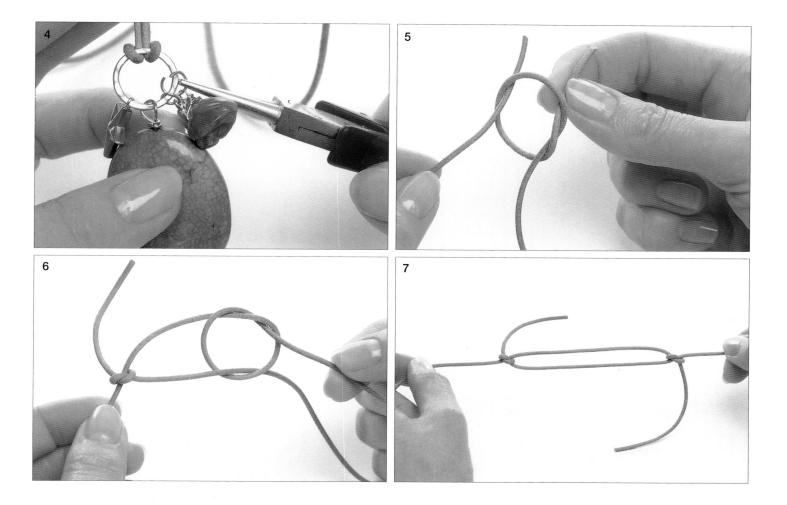

1 Loop the leather thong through the large closed jump ring.

2 Wire-wrap the large turquoise to the large closed jump ring.

3 Add the gold metal charms.

4 Wire-wrap the carved flower stones and attach with open jump rings. Add a small strip of chain with butterfly charm dangles. Cut the leather to whatever length you like.

5 Alternatively, create an adjustable knot: take one end of the leather and tie a square knot, so that one end ties around the other end of leather in an over-hand knot.

6 Repeat this on the other side of the leather. At the very ends of each end of leather, tie a stopper square knot.

7 Pull tight.

Tips

You can also finish the necklace with leather bead caps, which attach to a lobster clasp and jump ring.

Acrylic Flower & Ribbon Necklace

The delightful white flower beads in this fun necklace are knotted with sheer turquoise ribbon. White jewelry matches almost all outfits too!

Materials

A 14mm white flower acrylic beads x 5
B 12mm white flower acrylic beads x 10
C 10mm white flower acrylic beads x 10
D Turquoise sheer ribbon, approx. 2 yards

Tools

Scissors

Techniques

Knotting beads on ribbon.

1 Snip the ribbon at an angle and thread through the first small bead. Tie a knot on each side of the bead.

2 Add another four small beads, then five medium beads, followed by five of the larger size. Create a knot on each side after adding each bead.

3 Repeat on the other side of the necklace, adding five medium beads, followed by five small.

Tips

When planning the length of your necklace, remember to allow in your measurements for the extra ribbon used in the knots on each side of the beads. Do not cut the ribbon until you are happy with the length. Be sure, too, to check that your ribbon will thread through the beads you have chosen.

It is helpful, when planning your design, to lay out your beads on a mat.

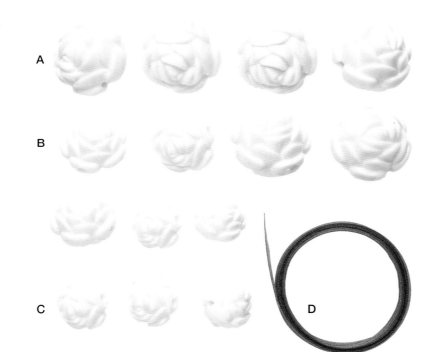

Three-Strand Cut-Glass Vintage Necklace

It is the unusual, twist-cut glass beads, which are a striking citrus-yellow color, rather than the design, that make this necklace so fabulous. Sometimes, less is more, and only by using a simple design can you truly appreciate the beauty and color of particular stones. This necklace is a great example, too, of how effective bead caps can be; they really do add to the completeness of the stones and work wonderfully as a decorative touch. The filigree of the bead caps also complements the vermeil clasp and give it a vintage feel.

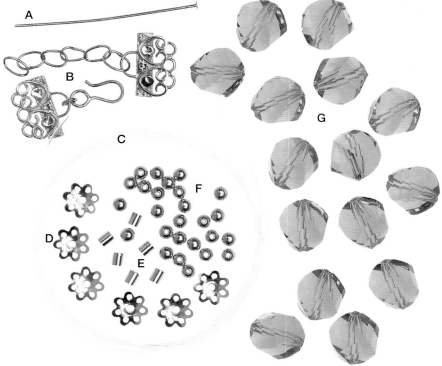

Materials

A Gold head pin
B Three-hole vermeil clasp
C Nylon monofilament, 2 yards
D Gold bead caps x 114
E Gold crimps x 6
F Gold spacer beads x 54
G 14mm glass, twist-cut beads x 115

Tools

Cutters or scissors
Chain-nose pliers or crimp tool

Techniques

Crimping nylon thread to clasps.
Working with bead caps and gold balls.

1 Thread a bead cap, then a glass bead, a bead cap, and a spacer bead on the nylon thread. Thread the first strand with approx 18 beads. Then add a crimp bead.
2 Loop the thread through the ring of the clasp and back through the crimp.
3 Press the crimp closed using chain-nose pliers. Snip the excess wire with cutters.
4 Repeat steps 1–3 to create strands 2–3.
5 Add a glass bead to the head pin, create a rosary loop at the top of the head pin and join to the clasp chain.

Tips

Each strand in multistrand necklaces should be slightly longer than the one before to give a perfect drape effect.

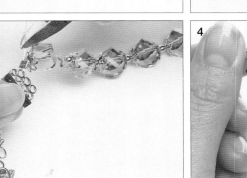

Tassel Necklace

This stunning statement necklace is fabulous to wear! The long fabric tassel adds another dimension and shows that you needn't confine yourself to traditional components when making jewelry. There are a lot of different beads in this design, though they are all of cream and golden tones. The tiny golden seed beads are particularly interesting because they have a delicate gold line through their middle.

Materials

A 28 gauge/0.4mm gold wire, approx. 1 yard
B 12mm AB Swarovski crystals x 12
C 6mm gold-lined cyrstal glass beads x 20
D Gold figaro chain, approx. 1 yard
E Cream satin tassel
F 12mm gold faceted metal balls x 9
G Gold seed beads x 1 small tube
H Oval-shaped two-tone cream and brown
firepolished beads x 30
I Gold beadcaps x 16
J Gold crimp beads
K Faceted smoky quartz rondels x 12
L Gold toggle clasp
Also:
Nylon monofilament, 3 yards

Tools

Chain-nose pliers
Scissors
Cutters

Techniques

Adding crimps to nylon thread to join beads and chain together.
Adding a fabric tassel.

How to make the tassel necklace

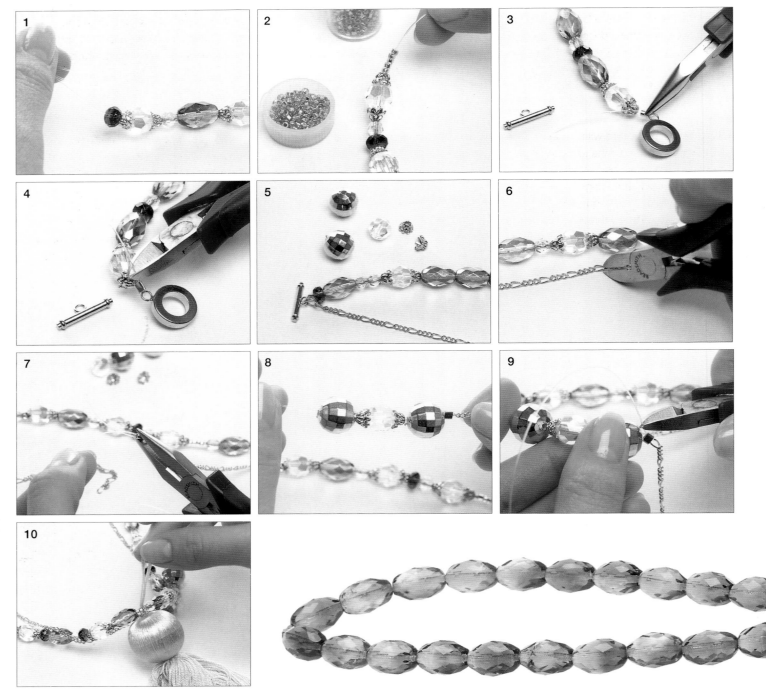

1 Randomly add your beads to the nylon thread. Try for a variation of beads, adding bead caps between crystal beads.

2 Add seed beads for a decorative touch.

3 Add a crimp bead to the nylon thread, then loop the thread through the O-ring clasp and back through the crimp bead. Press the crimp tightly shut with chain-nose pliers.

4 Snip the excess thread with cutters.

5 Take some gold chain the same length as your beaded necklace and attach it to the clasp with an open jump ring.

6 Cut the chain into four equal lengths.

7 Loop the nylon thread through one end of the chain. Add a crimp bead to the thread and press down firmly with chain-nose pliers to secure.

8 Add a trio consisting of a gold metal ball, a crystal oval and a gold metal ball. Secure this end with a gold crimp bead.

9 Snip the excess thread with cutters. Keep repeating these steps to add three beaded sections to the chain.

10 Find the center point of the necklace, and loop the tassel string around the necklace. You can add a touch of superglue to secure. Create a more decorative finish to the tassel by adding a strip of seed beads. Join the other end of the gold chain to the T-bar clasp to complete.

Tips

You may need to tidy up any stray strands from your tassel. As with any fabric component, it is a good idea to carefully spray the tassel with fabric protector first.

Variations

Below is a simpler, though still stunning, version of the necklace in warm blue and brown tones. Here the tassel is wrapped around a large quartz disk, which itself is wrapped with 8mm brown glass beads on nylon thread. To bring all the colors together, I have strung it on a necklace of beautiful, two-toned firepolished beads.

Rings & Trinkets

Rings & Trinkets

Having mastered the techniques in this book, it is possible to make a variety of fun accessories, such as the two styles of ring, bag charm, and brooch featured next.

Rings are increasingly popular in fashion jewelry design and the wide choice of ring components means they are particularly rewarding to make. Our second project actually teaches you how to make your own ring component. Bag charms can brighten up much-loved bags, and also look wonderful attached to key rings. Finally, another must-have accessory is a sparkly beaded brooch, which is guaranteed to add life to any jacket or coat.

Tiger-Eye Gold Ring

This ring base can be embellished with any type of stone. The tiger-eye used here is a fabulously rich stone with a black and brown luster to it. Although, for correct sizing, a ring sizer would be useful for this design, you can make do with a ring mandrel.

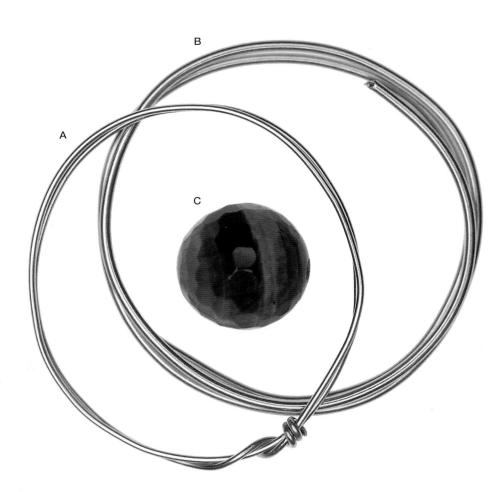

Materials
A 24 gauge/0.6mm gold-filled wire
B 18 gauge/1.0mm gold-filled wire
C 14mm tiger-eye round stone

Tools
Sturdy wire cutters
Ring mandrel
Chain-nose pliers
Round-nose pliers

Techniques
Creating ring components from wire.

Variations
This design works wonderfully with virtually any shape or type of stone. The variation, right, uses a beautiful turquoise stone.

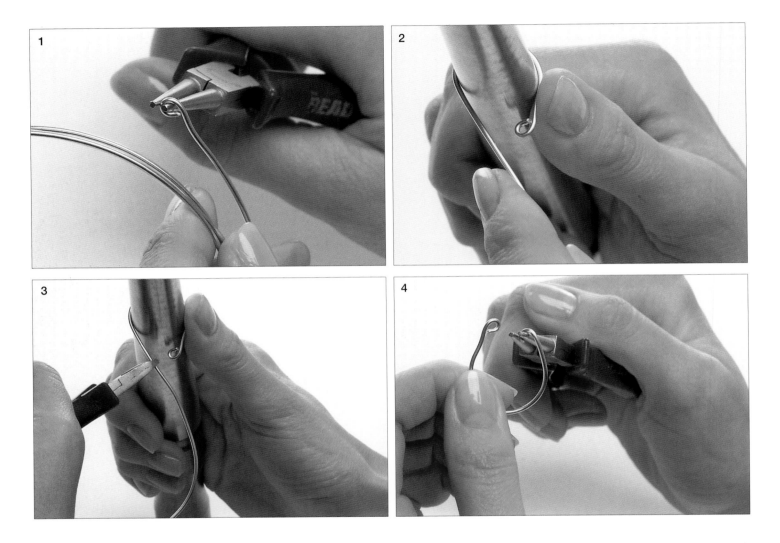

1 Create a loop in the wire with round - nose pliers.

2 Curl the 18 gauge wire around the mandrel.

3 Cut the wire with wire cutters.

4 Create a loop in the other end of the wire with round-nose pliers.

5 Using chain-nose pliers, turn the loops at an angle at both ends of the ring.

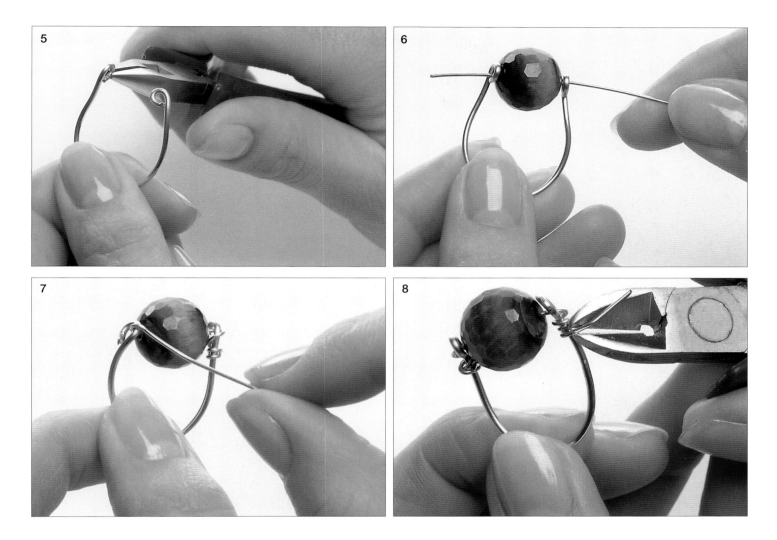

6 Take the finer, 24 gauge wire and loop it through the ring loop, then through the tiger-eye stone and finally through the other ring loop.

7 Wire-wrap the fine wire around the thicker wire to join them together.

8. Snip any excess wire with wire cutters.

Tips

Use a ring sizer to give you the correct size of ring you require.

Practice this design with base metal first before attempting it with gold-filled wire.

Crystal Cluster Ring

This fabulous crystal ring is guaranteed to attract a lot of attention. The slightly oversized 10 and 12mm round faceted crystals catch the light, adding sparkle and bling to this ring. The cube shape brings an unusual dimension, and the use of ball pins adds a decorative finish.

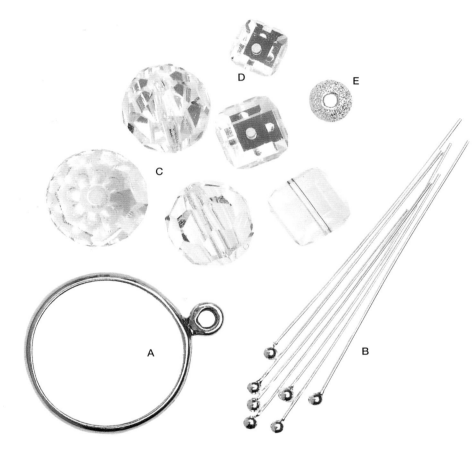

Materials

A One-hole sterling silver ring
B Sterling silver ball pins x 7
C 12mm and 10mm round AB crystals
D 6mm and 10mm cube crystals
E 6mm dusty silver ball x 1

Tools

Wire cutters
Round-nose pliers
Chain-nose pliers

Techniques

Working with ring components.

1 Add a ball pin to one large crystal.

2 Loop the pin onto the ring hoop and wire-wrap to the ring.

3 Continue to add the round and cube-shaped crystals to the ring hole.

4 Finally, add the 6mm dusty silver ball.

5 Try and have the different shapes mixed together.

Tips

Mix large and small stones when working with one-hole components.

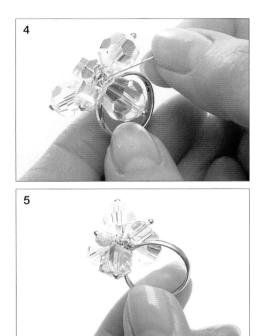

Variations

Gold and silver 10-hole ring variations of this design are shown on page 8. The gold design uses a stunning mix of padparadscha teardrops and bicones. The silver ring has 6mm blue AB crystals mixed with dusty silver balls.

Bag Charm

Bag charms are fabulous for re-vamping a handbag or for adorning a key ring.

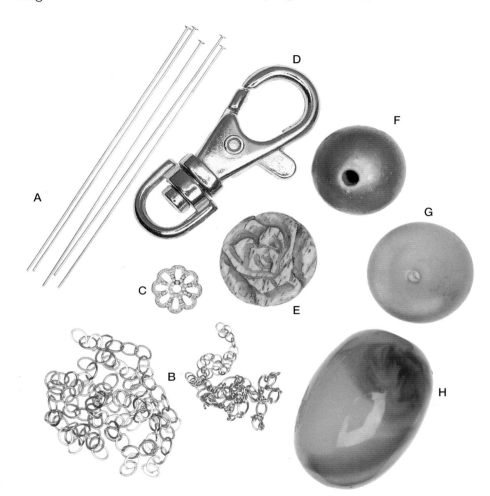

Materials

A Gold head pins x 4
B Strips of different fine chain
C Gold bead cap x 1
D Large key ring
E Carved flower bead
F 12 mm gold glass bead
G 10mm frosted bead
H Glass swirl bead

Tools

Wire cutters
Chain-nose pliers
Round-nose pliers

Techniques

Rosary-looping large beads to keyrings.

1 Using a head pin, add the flower bead to the large key ring.

2 Rosary loop the next two glass beads to the flower bead.

3 Add the large swirl bead to a head pin, followed by a bead cap. Create a loop in one end of the head pin and add the strips of fine chain to create your tassel.

4 Join the two beaded segments together.

Tips

Use cuts of chain to create tassels for a decorative finish to your bag charm.

Glass Beaded Brooch

Brooches add new life to jackets and coats and look fabulous. This one has a mix of seed beads, glass beads, and gold-lined 6mm glass beads. The finished design makes a stunning, sparkly brooch.

Materials
A 4mm two-toned glass beads x 15
B Brooch finding x 1
C Gold ball pins x 45
D 6mm gold-lined glass beads x 25
E Gold seed beads x 10
F Fine chain, approx. 6 inches

Tools
Wire cutters
Chain-nose pliers
Round-nose pliers

Techniques
Adding beads to brooch components.

Tips
There are many different brooch components available, so be sure to experiment with a few different styles to create a variety of brooches for your jewelry box.

Variations
You can add more tassels of chain to this design to give it some length.

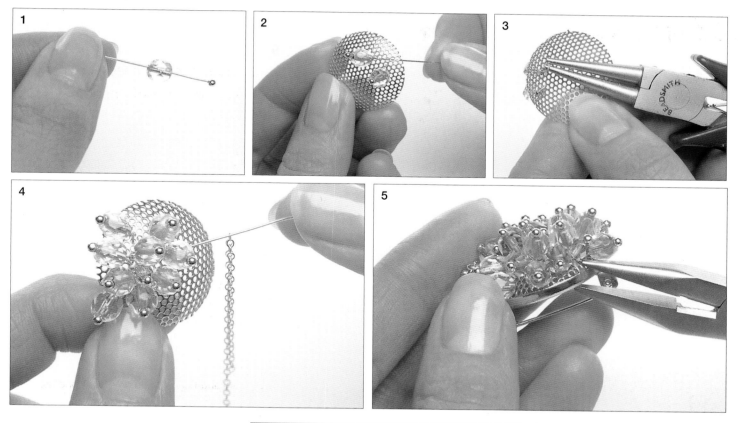

1 Add a glass bead to a ball pin.

2 Thread the ball pin through one hole of the brooch.

3 Cut the wire of the pin, then curl the pin to make a loop on the inside of the brooch. This loop will keep your bead in place.

4 Keep adding beads to your brooch. You can even add strips of chain to the pin before you add the bead. Add a mix of seed beads, 6mm glass and 4mm glass.

5 To close the brooch, use chain-nose pliers, and push the clips into place so the brooch is secure.

Suppliers

There are literally thousands of suppliers all over the world. To list each one would be impossible, but the following will get you started. Online bead stores are also appearing all the time, so search the internet, and eBay, which is a great source for beads and components. I would also recommend looking in local bead magazines for a list of suppliers in your area.

North America

Beadworks USA
www.beadworks.com

JKM ribbon USA
www.jkmribbon.com

Stitch and craft USA
ww.stitchncraft.co.uk

Fire Mountain Gems USA
www.firemountaingems.com

Rio Grande USA
www.riogrande.com

Rings and Things USA
www.rings-things.com

Brightlings beads USA
www.brightlingsbeads.com

Susies Beads USA
www.susiesbeads.com

Beads World USA
www.beadsworldusa.com

Art Beads USA
www.artbeads.com

Astral Beads USA
www.astralbeads.com/index.aspx

StoneAge Hardware USA
www.stoneagehardware.com

The Beading Room Canada
www.TheBeadingRoom.com

TheBeadGallery Canada
www.TheBeadGallery.ca

Austin Hamilton Canada
www.austinhamilton.ca

UK & Europe

The Bead Trail UK
www.thebeadtrail.co.uk

Beads Direct UK
www.beadsdirect.co.uk

Buffy's Beads UK
www.buffysbeads.com

Beadworks UK
www.beadworks.co.uk

Kernowcraft UK
www.kernowcraft.co.uk

Rashbel UK
www.rashbel.com

Jilly Beads UK
www.jillybeads.co.uk

The Bead Store UK
www.thebeadstore.co.uk

Bead Bazaar UK
www.thebeadbazaar.co.uk

Creative Beadcraft UK
www.creativebeadcraft.co.uk

Bead Addict UK
www.beadaddict.com/uk/index.htm

Barnet & Lawson UK
www.bltrimmings.com

International Craft UK
www.internationalcraft.com

Hobby Craft UK
www.hobbycraft.co.uk

Gems to Be Hold Europe
www.gems2behold.com

Perlen Paula Europe
www.perlenpaula.de

Beads and Co Europe
www.beads-and-co.com

Asia Pacific

ebeadsdirect Australia
www.ebeadsdirect.com/index.pasp

Unique Beads Australia
www.uniquebeads.com.au

Space trader Australia
www.spacetrader.com.au

The Bead Man Australia
www.thebeadman.com.au

Bead Needs Australia
www.beadneeds.com.au

Bead Box New Zealand
www.beadbox.co.nz

Beadworks Japan
www.beadworks.jp

Author's Acknowledgements

This stunning book was put together with the help of a number of very talented people. The research and attention to detail required for any technical piece of work takes tireless hours, and I could not have made the beautiful pieces of jewelry featured here without the help of my wonderful team, including Tracey Emery and Anne O'Niell, whose behind-the-scenes efforts have been incredible.

Thanks also are due to Lucy Gowans, who was remarkably patient during her crash course in jewelry design; Lucy has done a wonderful job in styling both the jewelry and the book. To Victoria Harvey, for lending us her lovely hands – far nicer to look at than any jeweler's hands. To Sian Irvine, for her photographic eye and talents, and for capturing the jewelry so beautifully. A big thank you to Jacqui Small for her clarity and vision, as well as Kate John and Judith Hannam for ensuring everything came together so well. Also to my husband, who is wonderfully patient and supportive.

I would also like to give special thanks to the following suppliers for contributing the beads and components that have helped make this book so special:

Barnet Lawson UK
Bead Addict UK
Beads Direct UK
Bead Trail UK
Beadworks UK and USA
Buffy's Beads UK
Creative Beadcraft UK
Jilly Beads UK
Swarovski Crystal UK